A WAY IN THE

WILDERNESS

KRISTEL ACEVEDO

An imprint of InterVarsity Press
Downers Grove, Illinois

InterVarsity Press
P.O. Box 1400 | Downers Grove, IL 60515-1426
ivpress.com | email@ivpress.com

InterVarsity Press® is the publishing division of InterVarsity Christian Fellowship/USA®. For more information, visit intervarsity.org.

Published in association with the literary agency of WTA Media LLC, Franklin, Tennessee.

Interior artwork by Adolfo Danilo Lopez.

Cover design: Faceout Studio, Jeff Miller
Interior design: Jeanna Wiggins
Cover images: DigitalVision via Getty Images: © naqiewei, © Nastasic, © ilbusca, © ZU_09; and E+ via Getty Images: © azndc, © denisk0

ISBN 978-1-5140-0928-4 (print) | ISBN 978-1-5140-0929-1 (digital)

Printed in Colombia by Editorial Nomos S.A. ♾

Library of Congress Cataloging-in-Publication Data
Names: Acevedo, Kristel, author.
Title: A way in the wilderness : meeting God in the desolate places of Scripture–a 6-week Bible study / Kristel Acevedo.
Description: Downers Grove, IL : InterVarsity Press, [2025] | Series: IVP Bible studies
Identifiers: LCCN 2024045564 (print) | LCCN 2024045565 (ebook) | ISBN 9781514009284 (paperback) | ISBN 9781514009291 (ebook)
Subjects: LCSH: Light and darkness in the Bible. | Bible–Study and teaching. | Bible–Devotional literature. | Christian life.
Classification: LCC BS680.L53 A34 2025 (print) | LCC BS680.L53 (ebook) | DDC 220.95–dc23/eng/20250113
LC record available at https://lccn.loc.gov/2024045564
LC ebook record available at https://lccn.loc.gov/2024045565

30 29 28 27 26 25 | 8 7 6 5 4 3 2 1

CONTENTS

Introduction • 1

How to Use This Book • 3

WEEK 1
The Wilderness • 7

WEEK 2
The Wilderness of Oppression • 31

WEEK 3
The Wilderness of Sin • 55

WEEK 4
The Wilderness of Distraction • 83

WEEK 5
The Wilderness of Despair • 107

WEEK 6
The Wilderness of Temptation • 135

INTRODUCTION

I often think about my "wilderness years"—six years when I felt confused, frustrated, and lost. For a while, I remembered those years with disdain. In fact, I didn't like remembering those years at all. I just wanted to put them out of my mind and forget. If you've ever walked through a difficult season, I bet you've had similar feelings.

Before we go on, you might ask, what exactly is the wilderness? Throughout Scripture we read about different people in the wilderness. They experienced a *physical* wilderness: a harsh environment where hardly anything grows, with just enough food or water to survive. Some fled to the wilderness because they had run out of options, as a last resort. Others found safety in the wilderness. Regardless, in each instance, we find that their experience in the wilderness was a time of preparation and growth.

You and I are unlikely to end up in a literal wilderness (unless you're the outdoorsy type). But most of us end up in a metaphorical wilderness at some point in life. It's a season when we may feel stuck and without options. We might feel directionless or even lost. It can also be a season of loneliness, isolation, or disconnection from others. And it is a season that feels particularly harsh. With little access to emotional or relational resources, we find ourselves weary and with little opportunity or desire for growth. And even though God is with us in the wilderness, we may feel as if he has abandoned us there.

Mother Teresa once described the wilderness experience as a "dark night of the soul," which was a phrase she borrowed from a poem by Saint John of the Cross, a sixteenth-century priest. Many others have referred to it as the "winter of the soul." Maybe you can relate to those descriptions.

My prayer for these next six weeks is that you will come to see how the wilderness, although difficult, is a place in which God meets us. Whether you've experienced a wilderness season in your past, are experiencing one now, or know someone else who has had just such an experience, this Bible study is written for you. But also for me (in fact, you might even say primarily for me). During my wilderness season, I felt alone and discouraged, and I thought God had forgotten me. Even after I came out of that difficult season, I felt only resentment for those years I thought were lost.

I understand the fear, distress, and isolation that comes with wilderness seasons, and I want to accompany you during this season. This Bible study is meant to encourage you with the biblical truth that we are never alone and that with God, even in a wasteland, nothing is wasted.

Throughout the next six weeks we will look closer at Adam and Eve, Elijah, Hagar, John the Baptist, even Jesus himself! That's right, Jesus also experienced the wilderness. We'll dig into the Scriptures and discover how the wilderness can shape us and form us. Most of all, we will remember that, regardless, God is always with us.

You can choose to engage with this study on your own, but my hope is that you will gather with a small group—hopefully in connection with your local church. I truly believe that we grow best in community. In community we share stories and hear different perspectives. And despite the brokenness the church has experienced, I still think she's beautiful and a great way to grow as a Christ-follower. The beauty of the church is in her diversity—men and women, different ethnicities and ages—all coming together to grow and live on mission. Let this study be a place where you can show up authentically as yourself and grow in Christlikeness together.

HOW TO USE THIS BOOK

Whether you are engaging in this study with a large group, a small group, in a coffee shop with a friend, or by yourself in your favorite chair, here are some helpful suggestions.

FOR THE GROUP SESSION . . .

Set aside a designated day and time for a weekly gathering—in person or virtually—for the next six weeks. The content (video and discussion) will take about an hour, but you can always allow additional time for a check-in or to share prayer requests.

Videos are accessed through the QR code in the book. These videos were created with a group in mind—that you would watch the video together and then immediately engage in the content that follows. But it also means that individuals have access, which is nice if someone has to miss a group gathering.

For the group discussion, take time to read the material together. Feel free to pause, ask questions, and share thoughts as you read. Take turns reading the Scriptures aloud and end your time in prayer.

A few tips on engaging in a group discussion:

1. Be willing to participate in the discussion. The leader of your group will moderate the conversation, and it helps them to have willing participants.
2. Be careful not to dominate the discussion. We are sometimes so eager to express our thoughts that we leave too little opportunity for others to respond. By all means participate, but also make space for the insight of others.
3. Be sensitive to the other members of the group. Listen attentively—you might be surprised by their insights!

4. When possible, link what you say to the comments of others. Also, be affirming whenever you can. This will encourage some of the more hesitant members of the group to participate.
5. Stick to the topic being discussed and try to avoid "rabbit trails."
6. Expect God to teach you through the content being discussed and through the other members of the group.
7. Pray that you will have an enjoyable and profitable time together, but also that as a result of the study you will find ways to take action individually or even together as a group.
8. Remember that anything said in the group is considered confidential and should not be discussed outside the group unless specific permission is given to do so.

It's important that we give space in this group to share authentically and that we hold each other's stories in confidence, not trying to fix anything, but trusting the Holy Spirit to do the work of healing and mending.

If you have time, a good check-in question might be to name a highlight from the last week of study—either from the group session or individual days. We designed these studies so that you could still participate in the group session even if you haven't done the homework, but—of course—we think you'll still want to engage with all the content on individual days!

FOR THE INDIVIDUAL DAYS . . .

Following the group session are five days of content for you to engage with on your own. This study is written with you in mind—so the content is meaningful but not overwhelming, and designed to fit into your normal everyday life.

A few tips for engaging in individual study and reflection:

1. As you begin, pray that God will speak to you through his Word.
2. Write your answers to the questions in the spaces provided or in a personal journal. Writing can bring clarity and deeper understanding.

3. Read the introduction to the study and respond to the personal reflection question or exercise. This is designed to help you focus on God and on the theme of the study.
4. Each study deals with a particular passage so that you can delve into the author's meaning in that context. Read and reread the passage to be studied. The questions are written using the language of the Christian Standard Bible, so you may wish to use that version of the Bible. The New Revised Standard Version is also recommended.
5. It might be good to have a Bible dictionary handy. Use it to look up any unfamiliar words, names, or places.
6. Use the prayer suggestion to guide you in thanking God for what you have learned and to pray about the applications that come to mind.

You'll notice that the group session starts the week, so your participation doesn't hinge on completing your homework. That being said, we want you to participate as much as you are able.

WEEK 1

THE WILDERNESS

Group Session

In our introduction, we describe the wilderness as a season of life in which you feel disconnected, lost, hurt, or confused. It is a season of spiritual dryness that can feel particularly harsh. Today I want to focus on the story of John the Baptist and look closer at the verse that challenged my perspective about seasons in the wilderness.

VIDEO

Watch the opening video.

OPENING ACTIVITY

People have used many words to describe wilderness experiences. These include:

- harsh
- lonely
- unintended
- dry
- terrifying
- hopeless
- barren
- desolate
- confusing

Take a moment to identify a wilderness season in your own life. It could be one you are currently experiencing or one you experienced in the past.

1. What difficulties, challenges, or heartaches brought you to the wilderness?

2. What words from the list above best describe your wilderness season?

During the rest of the week, we'll take a closer look at the life of John the Baptist. But for today we'll focus on the verse that changed my perspective on our wilderness seasons.

REFLECT

Luke 1:80 says, "The child grew up and became strong in spirit, and he was in the wilderness until the day of his public appearance to Israel."

What does it mean to be strong in spirit? Spiritual strength is not about digging deep or pulling yourself up by your bootstraps. Instead, it is reliance on and alignment with the Holy Spirit—it's a resilience that develops when we trust God to do the work in and through us.

3. Think of someone you know who is spiritually strong. What is an example of their spiritual strength?

4. In what area of your life do you tend to rely on your own strength rather than on God's strength?

Learning to rely on God's strength requires that we learn to trust God's character. Consider these words that God spoke through the prophet Isaiah:

> This is what the LORD, the King of Israel and its Redeemer, the LORD of Armies, says:
>
> I am the first and I am the last.
> There is no God but me.
> Who, like me, can announce the future?
> Let him say so and make a case before me,
> since I have established an ancient people.
> Let these gods declare the coming things,
> and what will take place.
> Do not be startled or afraid.
> Have I not told you and declared it long ago?
> You are my witnesses!
> Is there any God but me?
> There is no other Rock; I do not know any. (Isaiah 44:6-8)

5. List the titles and characteristics of God included in this passage.

6. What is God uniquely capable of accomplishing?

7. What reasons does this passage give us to “not be startled or afraid”?

8. How could recognizing God’s strength transform our perspective on our own spiritual strength?

9. What might God want to refine in you through the wilderness?

10. How is God preparing you now for the next season of your life?

In the coming days we will see how John the Baptist knew and lived with this conviction—that his strength came not from himself but from God.

PRAY

As you end this time together each week, I encourage you to spend some time in prayer:

Heavenly Father, our Rock and Salvation, the wilderness is not a pleasant experience. You know the pain we feel when wandering through it. We know, however, that you are with us in the wilderness. Not only do you give us your presence, you also give us your strength. Help us to walk in the power of your Spirit whether we are walking in the wilderness or sitting in the sanctuary. In Jesus' name, amen.

If time allows at the end of each group session, I encourage you to share with one another any prayer requests and bring them to our faithful and trustworthy God in prayer.

DAY 1

To move forward, it's important to look back. We touched briefly on John the Baptist's parents in the video, but let's take a deeper dive today.

READ & REFLECT

Read Luke 1:5-24

Zechariah and his wife, Elizabeth, both came from the priestly line of Aaron. They served God faithfully and humbly, and yet they remained childless. In this era childlessness was seen as a curse. Why God had not blessed them with children was beyond their understanding. At their age, however, Zechariah and Elizabeth probably expected no change in their situation and had learned to live with it.

Walking through infertility can be its own wilderness. While infertility may not carry the same stigma it did in biblical times, it's still frustrating and can cause women and men to feel that something is wrong with them. If that is your story, I grieve with you and I pray you would know your worth whether you have a child or not. I pray for supernatural comfort as you navigate this season of your life.

Zechariah is performing his priestly duties when he has a supernatural experience. An angel appears and delivers an incredible message.

Read Luke 1:5-17

- What do we learn about Elizabeth and Zechariah in verses 5 and 6?

- What is foretold to Zechariah by the angel?

- What is the significance of the angel's message for the people of Israel?

This is a pretty big deal! Not only will there be a child in their sunset years, but the child has a significant responsibility.

- How might have Elizabeth's and Zechariah's years of waiting for a child prepared them to raise a child with such a unique calling?

We can probably understand Zechariah's skepticism in his response to the angel: *How can this be? My wife and I are way past our prime.* Essentially, Zechariah is demanding a sign from the angel since he cannot comprehend how this message makes any sense.

Sometimes when we look at our circumstances instead of our God, we forget what is possible. Our circumstances may be limiting, but our God is limitless.

Indeed, Elizabeth does conceive and gives birth to a baby boy! And then when the baby is eight days old and Zechariah confirms that the boy's name should be John, Zechariah shares a prophecy. This passage is often referred to as Zechariah's song (Luke 1:68-79). As you look closely at this song, you'll notice that Zechariah makes declarations about God and about the new child.

- Think about your current circumstances—especially something that feels hard. What would it look like to view that circumstance through the filter of our God instead of the other way around?

Read Luke 1:57-79

- What does Zechariah declare about God? List those declarations below.

- In verses 76-79, he turns his attention to John. What is John's calling?

There had been no prophet among the Jews for centuries. Not only had Zechariah and Elizabeth dealt with unfulfilled longing in their childlessness, but the whole of Israel had been experiencing unfulfilled longing in their hunger for a Messiah. Now the time had finally come, Jesus was on his way, and John would be his hype man.

John would not save people because he didn't have the power to do so, nor was it his assignment. But he would call people to repentance and tell them about the One they had been waiting for, the One who could and would save them.

- As you consider times of waiting in your life, think of the people who stuck with you during those seasons. What truths did they remind you of? What disciplines did they invite you to practice? In what ways did they encourage you?

PRAY

End your time today in gratitude for the people in your life who have stuck with you in the wilderness seasons.

DAY 2

The arrival of John the Baptist ended more than four hundred years of prophetic silence. God's messages had been delivered by prophets for generations. After Malachi's ministry (around 400 BC), though, God seemingly went silent. But God had left a record of prophecy to encourage his people as they waited. One such prophecy told them to anticipate a new prophet who would prepare the way for the Messiah:

> A voice of one crying out:
>
> > Prepare the way of the LORD in the wilderness;
> > make a straight highway for our God in the desert. (Isaiah 40:3)

Yesterday, we read that hundreds of years after Isaiah, John's father, Zechariah, repeated this prophecy for his son.

READ & REFLECT

Read Luke 1:76-80

- What is similar about Zechariah's and Isaiah's prophecies? What is different?

- What evidence is there in verse 80 that these prophecies are being fulfilled?

John the Baptist is the one who would prepare the way for the Lord. Growing up with devoted, faithful parents, he grew strong in spirit and headed to the wilderness, where strength was tested and grew until he was ready to begin preaching.

Read Matthew 3:1-6

- What was John's life like in the wilderness?

- What reason does John give for baptism?

- How might John's life in the wilderness have prepared him for ministry?

The prophet Israel had been waiting for was hanging out in the wilderness. Maybe locusts are more delicious than I imagine, but that doesn't sound like an easy life. And his message was not an easy message: repent. *Repentance* is another word for turning or changing course. John's message was that Jews were going the wrong way—following the wrong things—and that they needed to turn toward God.

At my church, we often say that baptism is an outward expression of an inner transformation. Coming from a Roman Catholic family, I was baptized as an infant. I can't say I remember anything about that day, but I have seen pictures. My mom and dad were present along with my godparents, my Tía Nubia and Tío Henry. Tía Nubia held me in her arms as the priest poured water over my head.

Later, in high school, I began to consider my faith more seriously. I had been attending a Protestant church with friends and the topic of baptism came up. At first, I resisted any invitation to be baptized because I had already done that. I didn't want to reject my parents' baptism by having a "do-over." Over time, as I read Scripture and had conversations, I became convinced of the validity of believer's baptism by immersion. At the age of eighteen, after much prayer and discussion with my parents, I made the decision to be baptized again. The way I see it, my decision to be baptized affirmed my first baptism—a commitment from my own heart and mind to pursue Jesus, which is the desire my parents had for me all along.

- Getting baptized at age eighteen was my decision to repent and commit to following the way of Jesus. How might God be calling you now to repent and follow the way of Jesus?

- If you've not yet taken the step of repentance and baptism, take some time to pray and consider what this would look like for you.

- If you have taken this step, take some time to thank God for his faithfulness, for the salvation found in Jesus, and for the Holy Spirit's work in your life.

PRAY

If you heard John calling out for you to repent in order to get ready for Jesus' return, what might he be asking you to repent of? Take some time to write out a prayer of repentance.

DAY 3

Today I want to look at John the Baptist's story from a different vantage point—that recorded in the Gospel of John. Here we see a dispute arising from John's followers. They're upset because Jesus has begun his ministry and is also baptizing people. Rude! Doesn't he know that's John's deal?

READ & REFLECT

Read John 3:25-30

- How does John describe his role in relationship to Jesus?

John 3:30 includes a statement from John the Baptist that is frequently quoted in churches and youth groups. In fact, when I was a teen my own youth group had T-shirts with this phrase printed on the back: "He must increase, but I must decrease."

- Thinking about the relationship between John and Jesus, why would John "decrease" and what might that have looked like for him?

- If making room for Jesus to "increase" is the goal, what might it look like for you to "decrease"?

Decreasing can be difficult for those of us who get our sense of worth by increasing. But remember that before John the Baptist began his ministry, before he was even born, he was filled with the Holy Spirit. This filling helped him keep his eyes on his assignment. Although we are not told many details of John's upbringing, I can imagine that as he grew his parents reminded him of the words the angel spoke. I can imagine that as he walked the wilderness, this infilling of the Spirit helped him to remember his assignment and fulfill it.

Read Matthew 3:4-10

- How does verse 4 describe John?

- What did he tell the powerful Pharisees and Sadducees to do?

Following his assignment in the wilderness was not for the faint of heart, yet John, filled with the Spirit, remained steadfast in his ministry. When we partner with God in ministry, we too must choose to walk in the power of the Holy Spirit. How do we tap into that Holy Spirit power? By slowing down. Taking a beat. Listening. Immersing ourselves in Scripture. The still small voice? That's it.

When partnership with God brings us to the wilderness, we again must choose to walk in the power of the Holy Spirit. When others are confused about our assignment or try to change it, we choose to remain steadfast in the power of the Holy Spirit.

We are all called to ministry in some way, whether we work for a church, a bank, a law firm, or full-time parenting. We are each called to be ministers in our spheres of influence. When we take that calling seriously, we will experience adversity—we will have wilderness moments. And we can tap into the Holy Spirit power the same way John did. This is the essence of spiritual strength—reliance on and alignment with the Holy Spirit—and there is no better place to develop this strength than the desert.

PRAY

Occasionally in this study I will ask you to read and reflect on a psalm. The book of Psalms is a collection of 150 works of Hebrew poetry. The actual book of Psalms is further divided into five books filled with prayers and praises that were used in corporate worship. Furthermore, there are different categories of psalms. There are psalms of praise, psalms of thanksgiving, psalms of remembrance, and even psalms of lament.

These psalms, or prayers, were intended to guide worshipers. Have you ever felt like you don't have the words to express your feelings to God? The psalms can guide you in articulating your distress and then point you toward celebrating God's goodness and power.

As we end our time today, take a moment to breathe and focus on these words from the psalmist. Imagine John the Baptist praying these words as he ate locusts in the wilderness. Imagine him praying these words in the morning before a full day of baptizing people. Now pray it one final time for yourself.

> God, create a clean heart for me
> and renew a steadfast spirit within me.
> Do not banish me from your presence
> or take your Holy Spirit from me.
> Restore the joy of your salvation to me,
> and sustain me by giving me a willing spirit.
> Then I will teach the rebellious your ways,
> and sinners will return to you. (Psalm 51:10-13)

DAY 4

Unfortunately, John meets an untimely end. Speaking against Herod, he is arrested and put in prison.

READ & REFLECT

Read Matthew 14:1-13

- Why is Herod afraid to kill John?

- How did John's death affect his disciples? How did it affect Jesus?

By God's grace, this is not the end of John's story. Although John meets an untimely end, his ministry lives on. The book of Acts tells the story of the early church after the earthly ministry of Jesus ended. What I love about Acts is that it shows the impact of John's ministry as well as the interweaving of Jesus' ministry with his.

Read Acts 18:24-28

- How do verses 24 and 25 describe Apollos?

It is clear that John's ministry has had a lasting effect. This man, Apollos, was an Alexandrian, from Africa. Word of John's call to repentance and baptism had reached even there. And Apollos goes on to have an effective ministry traveling and preaching the gospel of Jesus Christ.

John's death and continued legacy is a humble reminder that the world we live in is suspended in an "already/not yet" reality. Sin still has influence in our world and sometimes terrible things happen.

I'm reminded of this when I turn on the news to hear of wildfires destroying homes or migrants stuck at the border or unjust governments taking advantage of citizens. There are many wilderness experiences and tragedies to mourn in our world.

- What unfortunate reality or wilderness experience are you mourning today? It could be something you saw on the news or something personal in your life. Take a few minutes to grieve and lay your burdens at the feet of Jesus. Write about it in the space below.

- How can knowing that John's legacy of ministry outlasted his tragic death encourage you as you mourn?

PRAY

End your time today by praying for God to give you eyes to see how the story ends despite any current difficult circumstances.

DAY 5

REFLECTION DAY

Lectio Divina (2 Corinthians 4:8-9)

On day five of each week we will have a "reflection day." We will rest from our study so we can pause and reflect on what God wants us to walk away with. For each of these weekly reflection days, I would like to introduce a spiritual practice that will aid in your contemplation. The goal is not to incorporate all of these practices into your daily rhythms. Rather, it is my hope to give you a taste of some different practices available so you can find one that fits with your personality and your season of life.

Today we will participate in the practice of *lectio divina*. *Lectio divina* is Latin for "divine reading." It's an ancient contemplative practice that helps us slow down and immerse ourselves in Scripture so we may have an encounter with God. This week we'll immerse ourselves in a passage from 2 Corinthians. While this passage was written after the life of John the Baptist, we can imagine it providing him with great comfort during his seasons of wilderness.

Find a quiet and comfortable space. Once you are seated and ready, breathe slowly and deeply. Ask God to meet you in this space and speak to you through the verses you are about to read. Remembering that our definition of spiritual strength is reliance on and alignment with the Holy Spirit, trusting God to work in and through us, use the guide below to immerse yourself in 2 Corinthians 4:7-9:

> Now we have this treasure in clay jars, so that this extraordinary power may be from God and not from us. We are afflicted in every way but not crushed; we are perplexed but not in despair; we are persecuted but not abandoned; we are struck down but not destroyed.

Lectio (read). This is your first reading of the passage. Read it slowly and prayerfully, opening yourself to the presence of God. You may want to read silently or aloud. Notice any words or phrases that jump out at you. Trust that God will bring to mind what he wants to emphasize. Allow for a time of silence after reading the passage.

Meditatio (reflect). On the second prayerful reading of the passage, focus further on the words or phrases that jumped out at you in the first reading. Reflect on why God would highlight these words to you. Try not to analyze the text too deeply, but rather receive what God has for you during this time. Ask him questions and listen for his response.

Oratio (respond). Read the passage for a third time, and then respond. This is your opportunity to respond to whatever it is the Father is inviting you to. You may find it helpful to record your response in a journal so you can go back and read it later. You can also simply pray aloud or silently.

Contemplatio (rest). The focus of the fourth prayerful reading is to rest in the love God has for you. You don't have to do or say anything. Let the Holy Spirit fill and refresh you. Sit in silence as long as you need.

We may be afflicted. We may experience trials. We may be confused. We may even be lost. But we are not crushed. We do not need to despair. We are not abandoned. And we're certainly not destroyed. We are being refined and conformed to the image of Jesus in preparation to fulfill his purpose in and through us.

WEEK 2

THE WILDERNESS OF OPPRESSION

Group Session

In week two of our study, we will turn our attention to a difficult subject—*oppression.* The reality of the world we live in is that many face oppression, an experience that bears all the hallmarks of the wilderness.

VIDEO

Watch this week's video. 

OPENING ACTIVITY

As we learned in the video, God saw and heard Hagar when she felt alone in the wilderness. To help you imagine the impact of that on Hagar . . .

1. Think of a time when you were seen by someone when you really needed it. What was the impact of that encounter?

2. Think of a time when you were *not* listened to. How did that affect you?

REFLECT

The author of Psalm 34 makes a powerful proclamation in verse 18: "The Lord is near the brokenhearted; he saves those crushed in spirit."

3. How have you felt God's presence when you have experienced discouragement or heartbreak? If you are willing, take one minute to share with the group as an encouragement to those who may be struggling to see God's activity in their life.

Read Genesis 16:4-15

4. What parts of Hagar's story affect you the most—positively and negatively?

5. How did Hagar respond to being forced to have Abram's baby?

6. How did Hagar respond to Sarai's mistreatment of her?

7. How did God meet Hagar when she was in the wilderness, "brokenhearted" and "crushed in spirit"? List everything the angel of the Lord does in verses 7-11.

What is the significance—then and now—of Ishmael's name? (Genesis 16:11)

8. What is the significance—then and now—of Hagar's name for God, El-roi? (Genesis 16:14)

9. How does the truth that God sees you bring comfort?

10. Knowing that God hears you, if you could ask him for one thing, what would it be?

As we go through the different days of the study this week, we will discover other stories of oppression from the Bible and from our modern world. Care for yourself well as we explore these stories. Lean on God to show you how he is at work.

PRAY

Faithful and trustworthy God, you are El-roi, the God who sees. You are also the God who hears. Your Word promises that you are always near and that your plan cannot be hindered. Remind us of this truth when we are going through our own struggles. Help us to see others as you see us. And help us to trust in you fully whether we are walking in the wilderness or sitting in the sanctuary. In Jesus' name, amen.

If time allows, share with one another any prayer requests and bring them to our faithful and trustworthy God in prayer.

DAY 1

Abram and Sarai (later renamed Abraham and Sarah) received a promise from God. This promise was that Abraham would have numerous descendants. But as the years dragged on, the promised children never appeared. Perhaps Sarai and Abram felt like they were in their own wilderness—feeling unseen and unheard by God as they waited for his promises to be fulfilled.

READ & REFLECT

Read Genesis 16:1-6

- How did Abram and Sarai respond during this time of waiting?

It seems that doubt crept in that God wouldn't keep his promise. The evidence? Sarah took matters into her own hands by giving Hagar, an Egyptian slave, to Abraham to produce an heir. In Week 1, we said that "spiritual strength is not about digging deep or pulling yourself up from your bootstraps. Instead, it is reliance on and alignment with the Holy Spirit—it's a resilience that develops when we trust God to do the work in and through us." Sarah's weakness here is striking.

- How can doubt sap our spiritual strength?

- When have you doubted God?

- How have your doubts about God affected your response to his guidance or his promises? How have your doubts affected how you pray?

- Rather than taking matters into their own hands, how might Sarai and Abram have developed their spiritual strength while waiting?

- Imagining that you are Sarai or Abram, write out how you might have prayed during this time.

Honestly, this story is hard for me to swallow. Abraham is supposed to be a "hero of the faith." Why isn't he stepping in? Why is he participating in this injustice? If you've ever been in a position where you experienced someone misusing their power or neglecting their responsibility, you know it's an incredibly difficult position to be in. I think about the many stories of spiritual abuse that have come out. Stories of pastors being bullies or taking advantage of women in their care. Stories of child abuse or neglect. It pains me, because that's not God's heart.

The one comfort I take in reading this story is that its inclusion in the Scriptures reminds me that the Bible is full of stories of real people—people who missed the mark and messed up. But all of their stories point to our good and great God who sees, hears, and knows us and remains faithful to all of his promises. The lesson I take from this story is that it's always a bad idea to try to accomplish God's will with human effort—this is spiritual weakness—and doing so can lead to disaster. It can even lead to abuse and injustice, as is the case with Hagar.

Abram and Sarai took their eyes off of God and decided to "help" him complete his promise. They forgot that God is faithful and does not need to be manipulated or maneuvered into fulfilling his promises. God is faithful; we are not. We will stumble and waver, but he never will.

PRAY

As we close today, prayerfully reflect on these questions:

- Who do we hurt when we take matters into our own hands?

- How can we keep our eyes on God and remember that he is faithful simply because of who he is and not because of anything we do?

DAY 2

Hagar, desperate and alone, has run away to the wilderness. In this dry and desolate place God meets her. The wilderness is often isolating and scary, especially when we find ourselves there because of mistreatment or oppression. Except Hagar wasn't technically alone—she was pregnant, which must have added to her fear.

When my *mamá* was pregnant with me, she and my *papá* had to flee their home country of Nicaragua. Civil war had broken out in the streets of their city and my dad was being targeted. Their lives were in danger. Like Hagar, they felt they had no choice but to flee. I can imagine not only the fear, but also the hope for a better life that drives someone to make such a risky decision—to willingly enter the wilderness, the lonely place of lostness and confusion.

For Hagar, the wilderness was a literal desert. For my parents, the wilderness was a foreign land where they knew no one, had no job prospects, and didn't speak the language. I'm sure the wilderness was the last place Hagar expected to meet God.

READ & REFLECT

Read Genesis 16:7-10

- What questions does the angel of the Lord ask Hagar?

- How does Hagar answer him?

God knows the answer to these questions, but he is asking because he wants Hagar to know he sees her, wants to have a relationship with her, and wants her to have agency to work out her thoughts and actions. He does the same for you.

- How would you answer the same questions God asked Hagar?

- Where have you come from?

- Where are you going?

Maybe you don't know the exact answers yet. After all, even Hagar only answered the first question while ignoring the second. That's okay. Giving ourselves time and space to examine where we are allows the Holy Spirit to work in and through us.

Read Genesis 16:11-15

When Hagar finishes her conversation with the Lord she gives God a name, El-roi, "the God who sees me." She is overwhelmed with the fact that God has seen her! Here's the thing that stands out to me. Nothing about Hagar's situation changed. God actually delivered a difficult message to her when he encouraged her to return to Sarai and raise her child in Abram's household. But something about her encounter with El-roi gave her courage and assurance.

Being seen is a tricky thing. On the one hand, we all want to be seen. No one wants to be ignored or relegated to the sidelines. On the other hand, sometimes being seen can be scary. What if we don't measure up? What if people notice all our mistakes or quirks or hang-ups? What if we get called to do something we don't feel equipped to do?

Ready for some good news? With God we are fully seen, fully known, and fully loved. God sees us, all of us, and loves every bit. You don't have to hide any of yourself because God already knows, and he loves all of you.

- What is something about yourself you are afraid of people seeing?

- How does it feel to be unconditionally loved?

This wasn't Hagar's last wilderness experience. If you live long enough, you will likely encounter multiple wilderness experiences. We'll explore Hagar's next wilderness experience tomorrow.

PRAY

Let's end today with a prayer:

You are El-roi, the God who sees. Thank you for being a good and gracious God who sees all of me and never leaves me alone. Give me eyes to see as well. Open my eyes to your Spirit's activity all around me. In Jesus' name, amen.

DAY 3

Years have passed since Genesis 16, and Abraham and Sarah (the new names God gave Abram and Sarai) have finally welcomed their son, Isaac, into the world. And once again we see the consequences of oppression. Sarah does not want Ishmael, Hagar's son, to grow up as a coheir with Isaac and tells Abraham to banish them to the wilderness.

Once again the people who were meant to care for Hagar and Ishmael are the same ones who discard them. Hagar does not run away this time; she is forced out.

READ & REFLECT

Read Genesis 21:1-19

- What does Abraham give Hagar and Ishmael for their journey?

- What happens when their provisions run out?

- How does God meet Hagar in the wilderness this time?

The Bible tells us Abraham is wealthy in livestock, silver, and gold (Genesis 13:2). So he certainly could have given Hagar and Ishmael riches, even servants, to go with them on their journey. But the oppression Hagar faced from Sarah and Abraham in the past continues as Abraham withholds the provisions necessary for survival while Hagar and Ishmael set up their new life.

But God has not forgotten Hagar and has not forgotten the promises he made her the first time she was in the wilderness. She may have doubted that he would fulfill those promises, but God still sees her, and this time he opens her eyes to see a well.

God provides for Hagar in a sweet and simple way. He helps her see she is not alone, even in the wilderness.

- In what ways have your eyes been opened during wilderness seasons?

- How have you experienced God in the wilderness in a way you might not have otherwise?

Read Psalm 23

Psalm 23 describes how powerfully we can experience God in the wilderness. This may be a familiar passage to you. It talks about God as our shepherd leading us through the wilderness—the valley of the shadow of death.

- List everything the shepherd does in this passage.

- How does the psalmist respond to all the shepherd does?

One way to build spiritual strength is to remember what the shepherd does for us when we are in the wilderness. We don't have to find green pastures or fill our own cups. We simply trust the shepherd and receive all he provides.

PRAY

End your time today by writing down the ways God has cared and provided for you. Thank God and save this list so you can look back on it and be reminded of God's care. If you are in a difficult season, adding even one thing to the list might be a challenge. Dear friend, know that God is with you, even in this valley.

DAY 4

We end Hagar's story by seeing that God does not abandon her or her son, Ishmael.

READ & REFLECT

Read Genesis 21:20-21

- In spite of Abraham and Sarah's abuse, how are Hagar and Ishmael flourishing?

Despite experiencing many setbacks, Hagar and Ishmael experience God with them. In fact, we see evidence here of him beginning to fulfill the promises he made to Hagar in chapter 16. Trusting God to fulfill his promises was difficult not only for Abraham, Sarah, and Hagar. The early church also struggled to trust God.

Read Galatians 4:21-26

Paul says the contrast between Hagar and Sarah is to be understood figuratively. With that understood, fill in the following chart.

	HAGAR	SARAH
Son's name?		
How was he conceived?		
Covenant from Mount Sinai or Jerusalem above?		
Under the law? (yes or no)		

Here the apostle Paul is instructing the church in Galatia about something very important, and he uses the story of Hagar and Sarah to illustrate his point. Many of the Galatians had been deceived and desired to be "under the law," probably because they believed their ethnic tie to the law made them righteous. Paul sets them straight though. He reminds them, "The son of the slave wife was born in a human attempt to bring about the fulfillment of God's promise" (Galatians 4:23 NLT). Abraham and Sarah attempted to act independently of God. They tried to take matters into their own hands and made a mess. Isaac, however, was born through supernatural intervention, a display of God's power and ability, a true fulfillment of his promise. This shows the promise of God versus human effort.

Paul uses this account as an illustration for the law and Christ—the old covenant and the new covenant. The Galatians wanted to live by the old covenant, but Paul demonstrates that God's covenant of promise with Abraham is fulfilled in Christ and his sacrifice. Now we who trust in Jesus are recipients of grace and freedom—true children of Abraham—free from obligations of the law, free to serve God. We are full heirs of the Abrahamic promise. This is what we gain as those who trust in God's promise rather than human effort.

- Even though we know we can trust God's promises, we often place our hope in human effort. Take a few moments to identify any places in your life you still find especially difficult to entrust to God.

- Thinking back on the life of Hagar—who faced oppression and other wilderness experiences—which of the following aspects of God's character do you most want to remember as you grow spiritually stronger, learning to trust God more and more?
  - ☐ God is with you in the wilderness, in the valley of the shadow of death, in the face of your enemies.
  - ☐ God sees you and hears your misery.
  - ☐ God asks you questions and gives you time to answer.
  - ☐ God opens your eyes to provision.
  - ☐ God is your shepherd who leads, guides, prepares, anoints, and provides for you.

PRAY

Write out a prayer of thanksgiving for this aspect of God's character. End it by asking God to help you trust him more and more as you face wilderness experiences in the future.

As we end our time today, join the psalmist in praising the Lord for all he does for the oppressed.

> Praise the LORD!
>
> Let all that I am praise the LORD.
> I will praise the LORD as long as I live.
> I will sing praises to my God with my dying breath.
>
> Don't put your confidence in powerful people;
> there is no help for you there.
> When they breathe their last, they return to the earth,
> and all their plans die with them.
>
> But joyful are those who have the God of Israel as their helper,
> whose hope is in the LORD their God.

He made heaven and earth,
    the sea, and everything in them.
    He keeps every promise forever.
He gives justice to the oppressed
    and food to the hungry.
The LORD frees the prisoners.
    The LORD opens the eyes of the blind.
The LORD lifts up those who are weighed down.
    The LORD loves the godly.
The LORD protects the foreigners among us.
    He cares for the orphans and widows,
    but he frustrates the plans of the wicked.

The LORD will reign forever.
He will be your God, O Jerusalem, throughout the
        generations.

Praise the LORD! (Psalm 146 NLT)

DAY 5

REFLECTION DAY

Prayer of Examen

We've come to the end of another week, and this wasn't an easy one. Stories of grief, tragedy, and oppression can weigh heavy on us as we sit with them. It's important that we care for our hearts well.

A practice I have started that helps me with this is the daily examen. This is a technique of prayerful reflection on the events of the day to notice God's presence and discern his direction. The daily examen is an ancient practice from Saint Ignatius that can help us see God's activity in our everyday life.

Sometimes, as with Hagar in the desert, it's easy to see God. Other times, as with Hagar's many years of slavery and wondering if God was ever going to rescue her and her son, it can be harder to see where God is at work. When we can't see God at work, it is more difficult to trust that he is our good shepherd who will fulfill his promises and lead us home. Examen helps us see God at work and build the strength needed to trust and follow God.

I find that examen is also helpful in identifying my emotions and bringing them to God, which is especially key when dealing with grief, as we have been this week.

There are many different versions of the prayer in circulation, but there are five basic steps:

1. ***Become aware of God's presence.*** First, create an environment where you can have an awareness of God. Make yourself comfortable. Slow your breathing. Calm your heart. Acknowledge that God is with you.
2. ***Give thanks.*** Look back on your day and give God thanks for anything you may feel grateful for. It could be the taste of your coffee, your family, no traffic on the way to work, good news from a friend. Anything.
3. ***Review the day.*** Look back on your day again, this time paying attention to your emotions. What stands out to you? When did you feel close to God? When did you feel far from God?
4. ***Respond.*** Talk to God about your day. Tell him how you felt. Ask him what he might be telling you through your feelings. Talk to God about whatever comes to mind.
5. ***Look ahead to tomorrow.*** Share with God what you are looking forward to and what you may feel anxious about. How do you want to enter into tomorrow?

Allow this prayer to still your heart, help you take notice of God, and center you on Jesus.

WEEK 3

THE WILDERNESS OF SIN

Group Session

Adam and Eve were the first to experience the wilderness in Scripture. Throughout this week, we will see why they were in the wilderness and how God cared for them even when they didn't trust him. It's God's kindness that leads to repentance and transformation.

VIDEO

Watch this week's video. 

OPENING ACTIVITY

I mentioned in the video that I love plants and try to imagine just how beautiful Eden must have been. This also makes me wonder what the wilderness outside of Eden was like. What did Adam and Eve see when they left the garden? In the space designated, take five minutes to draw pictures or list words that help you imagine both Eden and the wilderness.

EDEN	WILDERNESS OUTSIDE THE GARDEN

1. As you look at each side of the space above, what word or phrase best captures your life today? (You may have elements of both sides.)

REFLECT

Read Genesis 1:26–2:3

2. What characteristics of God do you notice in this passage?

3. How does God provide for Adam and Eve?

4. Why is it significant—both for God and for us—that God rests?

Last week we explored how doubt can sap our spiritual strength, making it harder to trust God. Here we see Satan planting those seeds of doubt. The start of his question, "Did God really say . . . ," calls into question God's goodness.

5. How do the serpent's words call into question those characteristics of God you identified above?

6. Keeping in mind God's characteristics, how might Eve have responded to the serpent?

7. Consider an area of your life where you need to trust in God's goodness. If the serpent were standing in front of you right now, trying to tempt you to doubt God, how might he finish the question "Did God really say . . . ?" How might you respond?

Read Psalm 111:7

8. What does this verse say about the works of God's hands? About his instruction/commands?

9. Why are God's commands trustworthy?

10. What do you find trustworthy about God's commands?

11. Where is the Holy Spirit leading you to trust God more fully?

A caution here: doubt itself is not a sin. When we bring our doubts to God—even doubts about him—it means we are genuinely seeking him. And God always honors that sort of genuine seeking.

PRAY

Pray to end your time together. You can use the prayer below or come up with your own:

Faithful and trustworthy God, thank you for your lovingkindness. From the beginning of Genesis, your character is on display. You created humanity out of the abundance of your love—you created humanity in your image. Your intent has always been to provide for your creation, and we see that most clearly in Jesus. As we begin this study, help us, through the power of your Spirit, to build the foundation of trust in our relationship with you. Help us to remember your goodness. In Jesus' name, amen.

If time allows, share with each other any prayer requests and bring them to our faithful and trustworthy God in prayer.

DAY 1

In this week's group session, we explored how the serpent tempted Adam and Eve to doubt God's goodness, causing a breach in their relationships. Today we're going to back up a bit to look at how those relationships started out.

READ & REFLECT

Read Genesis 1:26-27

- List all of the repeated words in these verses. (Feel free to include words that mean the same thing.)

All of humanity is created in the image of God—the *imago Dei*. To be made in God's image implies inherent dignity and worth for all people. To be made in God's image is a biblical designation for humanity's unique nature, status, and worth among all of God's creation. No other creature carries the image of God! That's pretty special.

To be made in God's image also implies that we are created for relationship with God—we have the ability to relate to God in a unique way that is different from the rest of God's creatures.

- When we accept that we are made in God's image and that God desires a relationship with us, what does that tell us about God's character?

The Bible is God's story because it reveals to us who God is and what he has done. As we read the Bible, one of the best questions we can ask ourselves is, *What can I learn about God's character from this passage?*

Read Genesis 1:27-29 and 2:16-17

- In these verses, what are Adam and Eve responsible for? What is God responsible for?

- When we read about the terms God set with Adam and Eve in Genesis 1 and 2, what do they tell us about God's character?

The fact that God offers responsibilities to Adam and Eve tells us a lot about how God sees humanity. We are not simply puppets; we are co-laborers. God trusts us to be stewards of the resources he provides. Work is an essential part of human dignity. We all have inherent dignity and worth because we all bear the image of God. This is a beautiful and intimate reality. God loves you. God cares about you. God offers us an intimate relationship with him and a purpose to live out in this world.

Not only are we created for relationship with God, we are also created for relationship with other people.

Read Genesis 2:18-25

- How did God attempt to find a helper for Adam in verses 19-20?

- When that did not work, how did God find a helper for Adam in verse 21?

- What do verses 23-25 identify as the hallmarks of this ideal human relationship?

It's almost like you can hear the tires of a car skidding to a halt in verse 18. Until now, God had looked at all he made and "saw that it was good." Verse 18 is the first time God declares something "not good." What happened?

Everything was good, and now all of a sudden it's not? Adam is surrounded by the beauty of Eden—rivers, plants, and trees. He is also surrounded by animals, which are also good! But those animals don't offer Adam companionship or partnership. Which means Adam is "alone." And it is not good for Adam to be alone. So God creates a counterpart for Adam.

When Adam sees her, he says, "This one, at last, is bone of my bone" (Genesis 2:23). Even in the beauty of Eden, Adam knew that something was missing. While this passage is often used to speak about marriage, the bigger message here bears repeating: *It's not good to be alone*. We are created to be in relationship with one another.

When we say humans are made in the image of God, a significant aspect of that reality is our relational capacity—humans are designed for relationship with God and for relationship with others. Tomorrow we'll think more about how sin has affected those relationships, but for now let's take a look at a conversation Jesus had with a religious leader about those relationships.

Read Matthew 22:34-40

You are familiar with the Ten Commandments, and you might also be aware that God offered more instructions for his followers in the Old Testament. But you may not know that the Pharisees—a group of religious leaders during Jesus' day—added several more rules of their own (about food, the Sabbath, cleanliness, and so on) in order to be considered the most faithful to God. And when it was all added up, it made for a list of over six hundred laws.

- Of all the laws (commands, commandments, rules, and guidelines), what does Jesus identify as the most important?

In Genesis we learn we were made for relationships with God and with others. And Jesus' response to the religious leader reminds us what those relationships should be marked by: love.

PRAY

As you close your time today in prayer, consider praying these words of the psalmist:

> When I look at the night sky and see the work of your
> fingers—
> the moon and the stars you set in place—
> what are mere mortals that you should think about them,
> human beings that you should care for them?
> Yet you made them only a little lower than God
> and crowned them with glory and honor.
> You gave them charge of everything you made,
> putting all things under their authority—
> the flocks and the herds
> and all the wild animals,
> the birds in the sky, the fish in the sea,
> and everything that swims the ocean currents.
>
> O LORD, our Lord, your majestic name fills the earth! (Psalm 8:3-9 NLT)

God knows us and God makes himself known to us. That's a remarkable truth worth contemplating.

DAY 2

READ & REFLECT

Read Genesis 3:1-7

- Which three characters are present for this conversation?

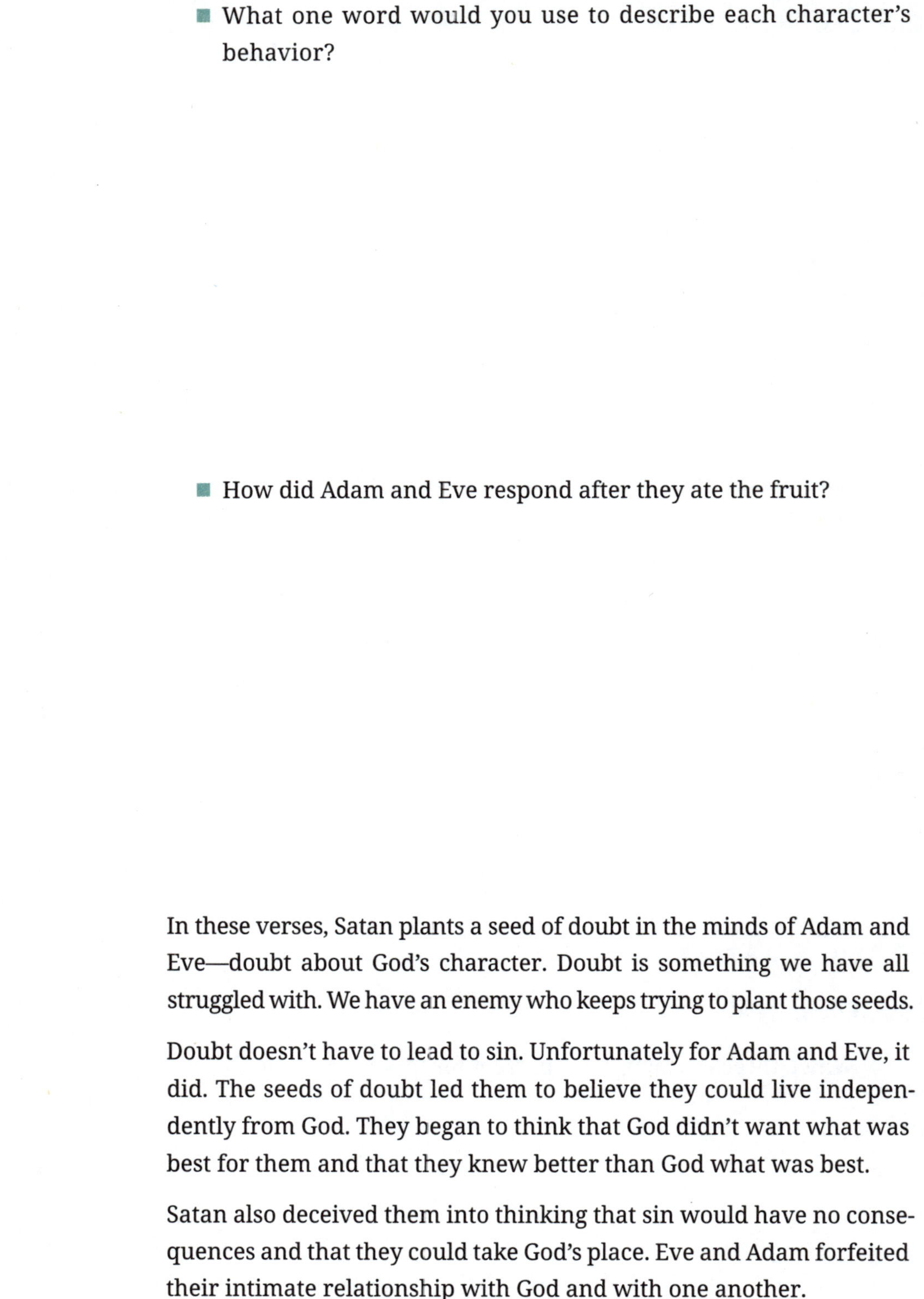

- What one word would you use to describe each character's behavior?

- How did Adam and Eve respond after they ate the fruit?

In these verses, Satan plants a seed of doubt in the minds of Adam and Eve—doubt about God's character. Doubt is something we have all struggled with. We have an enemy who keeps trying to plant those seeds.

Doubt doesn't have to lead to sin. Unfortunately for Adam and Eve, it did. The seeds of doubt led them to believe they could live independently from God. They began to think that God didn't want what was best for them and that they knew better than God what was best.

Satan also deceived them into thinking that sin would have no consequences and that they could take God's place. Eve and Adam forfeited their intimate relationship with God and with one another.

Although they have not yet been exiled from the garden, they experience some of the characteristics of the wilderness almost immediately. You may remember from the introduction that the wilderness can be a season of loneliness, isolation, or disconnection from others. Aware that they are naked and feeling ashamed, Adam and Eve cover up with fig leaves and hide from God. This pattern is one most of us are all too familiar with.

I'm a mom of two kids. I'm not a perfect mom by any means, but I try to show my kids love and grace. I have always told them that if they do something wrong, they should come to me and I will help them navigate any difficult circumstance they find themselves in.

Of course, my kids aren't perfect either. They have gotten themselves into some tough spots. Once my son was caught doing something he shouldn't have, and then he had the audacity to lie about it. No, he didn't rob a bank or anything—after all, he was just starting middle school—but nonetheless I was saddened by his choice. He hid from me and tried to talk his way out of it. He pointed fingers and tried to blame others. I felt incredibly frustrated by his actions. Why did he hide? Why couldn't he tell me? Didn't he believe I loved him and wanted the best for him?

As I lamented my son's actions with a friend, she reminded me of Adam and Eve. They were loved by God perfectly and unconditionally, and yet they chose to hide too. How much more would my son hide from me, a very imperfect mother? I began to feel compassion for my son, who was struggling with shame and fear.

- When are you most likely to experience shame? How do you sew fig leaves, cover up, or hide?

Thankfully, God doesn't want to leave us in the wilderness of shame. Tomorrow, we'll learn about God's plan to care for Adam and Eve. Today, we'll look at his plan for us.

Read Romans 5:8

- According to this verse, what two things led to Christ's death?

We don't have to buy into the lie that when we mess up, God is no longer interested in a relationship with us. We don't need to take care of it, clean ourselves up, and make ourselves good before God will see us, know us, or want us. That's not how God does things.

Romans 8 reminds us that Jesus Christ died for sinners. God loved us even in our sin. We don't need to sew up fig leaves; God has something better for us. He provides Jesus as a sacrifice for our sin.

We have been declared righteous, meaning we are made good and holy, set apart. When God looks at us, he sees Jesus. As we read on in Romans, we learn that we have received reconciliation. That means our relationship with God has been restored, just as he intended—we are no longer sinners, but saints.

At my church we envision the cross as we think about reconciliation and relationship. Through reconciliation with God (picture the vertical beam of the cross for this), we are given a path to reconciliation with others (think of the horizontal beam). Still, our relationships still experience the strain of sin today.

PRAY

End your study today by writing a prayer. In this prayer, thank God for the reconciliation we get to experience through Jesus. Focus your attention not on your own sin, but on the greatness of who God is. Look to Psalm 32 for inspiration.

DAY 3

Growing up, I didn't have a good grasp of the concepts of grace and mercy. In my eyes, the world was black and white, and when you messed up, disappointment and shame were sure to follow. Grace, however, is receiving something good you don't deserve, and mercy is not receiving punishment we do deserve.

The story of Adam and Eve being driven from the garden grieved my heart. On the one hand I shook my head and said, "Yeah, they deserved that." On the other hand I felt bad for Adam and Eve and wondered why God didn't just give them another chance before sending them off into the wilderness. Where was God's grace and mercy for Adam and Eve?

READ & REFLECT

Read Genesis 3:8-24

- What is God's response to Adam and Eve hiding (verses 8-9)?

- What consequences does God give the serpent, Eve, and Adam (verses 14-19)?

- Why do you think God made clothing for Adam and Eve?

God could have, of course, wiped Adam and Eve out and started over. Perhaps the next humans would be more trusting and obedient. Instead, in his mercy, he allows them to live and continue in relationship with him, even if that relationship will be far less intimate going forward.

Then there is the incredible grace of the animal-skin coverings, a gift they did not deserve. When Adam and Eve's eyes were opened, they immediately took fig leaves to cover their nakedness. In his kindness, God offered them better coverings that wouldn't fall apart, coverings that would protect their skin from the thorns and thistles of the wilderness they were about to enter.

These coverings, though, would require God to sacrifice his beloved animals. From that point on, throughout the Old Testament we see that the animal sacrificial system developed as a means for covering sin. Finally, in the Gospels, we see Jesus as the final sacrifice.

- How do you feel about the consequences Adam and Eve received? Do they feel just? Merciful?

- What sort of metaphorical "animal-skin coverings" has God provided when you felt ashamed and wanted to hide?

In Leviticus 23:26-32 God established the Day of Atonement. On this day Israel would collectively turn away from sin and toward repentance. A symbolic payment would occur for the collective sin of Israel, and as a result, purification would take place. This would allow for God's presence to remain with God's people while maintaining God's divine justice. God called his people to holiness, and he was good enough to provide a way to that holiness.

But this ritual, and all the other sacrifices the people needed to make to atone for their sins, were only a shadow of things to come.

Read Hebrews 10:1-10

- Why were the animal sacrifices—sacrifices required by the law—insufficient?

Jesus is the final and eternal Day of Atonement. This is the great mercy we receive in the wilderness. We don't have to clean up our act or get our lives together. We don't have to continually offer sacrifices in order to be purified. Forgiveness is already ours. Part of growing spiritually strong is recognizing sin for the wilderness it is, repenting of that sin, and walking in the freedom we have received in Christ.

PRAY

As we close our time together today, consider praying these words from the psalmist:

My soul, bless the LORD,
and all that is within me, bless his holy name.
My soul, bless the LORD,
and do not forget all his benefits.

He forgives all your iniquity;
he heals all your diseases.
He redeems your life from the Pit;
he crowns you with faithful love and compassion.
He satisfies you with good things;
your youth is renewed like the eagle.

The LORD executes acts of righteousness
and justice for all the oppressed.
He revealed his ways to Moses,
his deeds to the people of Israel.
The LORD is compassionate and gracious,
slow to anger and abounding in faithful love.
He will not always accuse us
or be angry forever.
He has not dealt with us as our sins deserve
or repaid us according to our iniquities. (Psalm 103:1-10)

DAY 4

We read at the end of Genesis 3 that after God drove Adam and Eve out of the garden, he placed cherubim at the entrance to keep them from returning. While that may seem cruel on a first reading, think about what would have happened if he hadn't: Adam and Eve may have eaten from the tree of life and lived in their fallen state forever. Instead, mercifully, God sent them into the wilderness where they would one day no longer be subject to the harsh world, broken human relationships, and broken relationship with God.

Today we will look at the wilderness we all now live in. And we'll see God's incredible grace to us, even when things are very, very broken.

READ & REFLECT

Read Genesis 4:1-10

- Throughout this passage, where do we see evidence of God at work?

- How do humans relate to God here?

With the Lord's help, Eve gives birth to two sons. The birth of children is usually a joyous occasion. As the mom of two kids myself, I have always dreamed of my kids being best friends and loving each other through the highs and lows of life. I wonder if Eve had those same desires.

In Genesis 4:3-4, Cain and Abel present their offerings to the Lord. God has regard for Abel's offering but not for Cain's. The text isn't explicit on why this is, but we can see clues in the Scripture. We are told that Abel gives the "firstborn" of his flock, while Cain gives "some" of the produce. It could be the attitude with which Cain presents his offering that causes God not to have regard for it.

Further evidence for Cain's poor attitude is shown in verse 5—Cain becomes furious.

- What is your response when you are confronted about your sin?

Cain's response—becoming defensive and angry—is relatable, isn't it? Just like doubt, anger is not necessarily sin; it's what you do with it. God tells Cain, "Sin is crouching at the door. Its desire is for you, but you must rule over it" (Genesis 4:7). Cain has a choice here, just as Adam and Eve had a choice. Like Adam, Cain can choose to worship and obey God or live independently from God and God's best. Cain's self-absorbed emotions manifest as murder when he lures his brother into a field and kills him.

Here we are introduced to the cycle of sin. Over and over again in the Old Testament we see this cycle continue. When I was a new Christian, I started dating a young man. We were both naive and immature. Unfortunately, we fell into unhealthy patterns. Not only were we engaging in sexual sin, we also had conflicts that ended in screaming matches and, on some occasions, physical violence. It was awful. I knew it wasn't God's best for my life, but I felt stuck.

It took me a long time, but eventually God revealed that I was not shackled to sin.

- Do you ever feel like you're stuck in a cycle of sin? Is there one particular sin that you can't seem to "master"?

Read Genesis 4:11-16

- How does God show Cain mercy even amidst his judgment?

God was present with Adam and Eve's family in the wilderness—graciously allowing them, at least in part, to fulfill their purpose as those who would fill and steward the earth. And he was there to protect them from some of the worst consequences of their sin. Eventually, through Jesus, God offered humanity a complete and permanent way out of the wilderness we find ourselves in as a result of sin.

Read Romans 6:1-11

Fill in the chart below with everything this passage says about our old lives versus our new lives in Christ.

OLD LIFE	NEW LIFE

Since we have been raised with Jesus to new life, we no longer have to allow sin to rule us. The cycle of sin has been broken by the sacrifice Jesus made on the cross. We are no longer slaves to sin. Of course, we still live in a broken world, and this is a process. Although we have been set free from the penalty of sin, we are still being freed from the power of sin, and one day will be freed from the presence of sin. As we develop spiritual strength, we will be able to say no to sin more easily, and we will be quicker to repent if we do sin.

Just ask my husband! In the beginning of our marriage, our fights were epic. As time has gone on, though, and we have developed in our faith, we are quicker to come together after a disagreement, quicker to show grace, quicker to find a compromise. It's not that we never argue; it's that more often than not, we fight for each other instead of against each other.

That's how it is with sin. We may still struggle, but Jesus has won the victory over sin. And one day sin will be completely vanquished.

PRAY

As you end your time of study today, pray the prayer below as a reminder of your freedom from sin:

God, thank you for the freedom you have given me from the power of sin in my life. When I find myself caught in the cycle of sin, remind me of the new life I have in Christ. I am dead to sin and alive in Christ. In Jesus' name, amen.

DAY 5

REFLECTION DAY

Journaling

We're at the completion of another week together, and I want to invite you to take a breath. I like to end the week nice and easy—curled up with a warm cup of coffee and my favorite blanket. I also have a special journal I like to write in. I love journaling and have boxes of old notebooks filled with my thoughts and prayers (and truthfully, I hope no one ever reads those!). Journaling helps me to process and talk to God in a way that is more focused. And it's nice to have something I can look back on to remind me how God has met me in the past.

On this day for rest and reflection I want to take you to Luke 15:11-32. This is one of my favorite chapters in the Bible—one I've read over and over again. Each time I read the parable of the lost son, it fills me with hope.

Read Luke 15:11-32

In this beloved story, a man has two sons. The younger son asks for his inheritance and leaves. He squanders his money and is reduced to working on a pig farm—certainly an unworthy line of work for a Jewish person. When the young man comes to his senses, he decides to return home from the far country, where he has been wandering in his own wilderness, to his father. He plans out a speech of repentance and practices it before returning. From a distance, the father sees his son and is overcome with joy. The father leaps to his feet and runs towards the son he thought was lost forever. We see here the divine initiative to seek and welcome sinners toward repentance.

Before the son can get his speech out, the father calls for a celebration: "This son of mine was dead and is alive again; he was lost and is found!" (Luke 15:24).

Salvation is not about going from "bad" to "good." Salvation is moving from death to life. In the parable, the son's status is fully restored. The same is true for us. We are now children of God, fully alive in Christ Jesus and empowered by the Spirit to live a life of holiness.

Today I invite you to reflect on Luke 15—and the story of the lost son in particular. Take some minutes to journal your thoughts on what this passage means to you. As you do, ask God to search your heart and repent of any sin you may be holding on to. The wilderness of sin doesn't have to be full of despair. We have hope for repentance and restoration because God meets us there.

If you want, select one of the following journaling prompts to get you started:

- How has each of the sons, in his own way, found himself in the wilderness, cut off from the love of the Father?

- Which character in this parable do you most identify with? Why?

- In what ways have you strayed from God and how is he calling you home?

- Reflect on God's forgiveness in your life.

- Write about a time when you were able to forgive someone and how it changed your relationship with them.

WEEK 4

THE WILDERNESS OF DISTRACTION

Group Session

Distraction is a chief problem in our world today. It seems like all around us, different voices are calling for our attention. This week we will learn how to turn down the noise of life and turn up the volume of God's voice. When distractions come our way, we can stay focused on Jesus.

VIDEO

Watch this week's video. 

OPENING ACTIVITY

In this week's video I describe how my husband gets distracted. If someone were observing you for a day, how would they describe the ways you get distracted? Choose one of the following prompts to complete. Then take a minute to share your response with the group.

1. On my way out the door to pick up last-minute items from the grocery store, I . . .

2. When I open up my computer to write an important email, I . . .

3. As I sit down to read my Bible (or pray), I . . .

REFLECT

As the book of Exodus begins, we see God initiating a daring plan to rescue his people, the Israelites, from slavery in Egypt. The Israelites were groaning from the oppression, and Exodus 2:24-25 says, "God heard their groaning, and God remembered his covenant with Abraham, with Isaac, and with Jacob. God saw the Israelites, and God knew." God noticed the suffering of his people.

When Scripture says God "remembered" the promise he made to Abraham—to make him the father of many nations and to bring the Messiah through the Israelites—this does not mean God ever forgot. "God remembered . . . " is a phrase used throughout the Bible as a literary device to assure the reader that God is delivering on his promise.

God heard and remembered the Israelites and helped them escape from bondage. But then, just as they were about to make their way to the Promised Land, they found themselves in the wilderness with a sea on one side and the murderous Egyptians on the other. As my kids say, "The math is not mathing."

Read Exodus 14:10-14

4. As the Israelites stand on the shores of the Red Sea, what do they focus on?

5. What feelings do they experience?

6. What does Moses invite them to focus on?

7. How would that affect their feelings?

Yes, God is faithful to keep his promises. But it can feel all but impossible to believe that when we are being attacked. Instead we are distracted by our enemies. We take our eyes off of God and forget all about God's faithfulness. While we get distracted, though, God never does. And he uses Moses to remind the people of this important truth:

The Lord will fight for you.

And then he uses Moses to part the sea.

Read Exodus 15:1-20

8. What is the response of the Israelites after God has freed them?

9. What adjectives and verbs do the Israelites use to describe God?

10. Think of a time when you experienced a moment of worship after an intense experience that required you to trust God.

11. How did that experience affect your relationship with God?

PRAY

Take five minutes to write a short prayer of thanksgiving modeled after Moses and Miriam's song:

- Sing to the Lord, for he is highly exalted. (Fill in what God has done for you.)

- In the greatness of your majesty, you . . . (Fill in how God has come to your rescue.)

- Who is like you? (Describe God.)

- The Lord reigns forever and ever.

When everyone is finished, let volunteers read their song aloud. If time allows, share with one another any prayer requests and bring them to our faithful and trustworthy God in prayer.

DAY 1

Do you like road trips? The truth of the matter is, I do not. That's because I would like to get from point A to point B as quickly as possible! We live in South Carolina, but our families are in Miami. Every time we plan a trip to visit our beloved hometown, I beg my husband to put up the cash for airline tickets. The alternative being twelve hours in a car packed with suitcases and two bickering children. No thank you! Just get me on a plane and get me to my destination as quickly as possible!

The Israelites were no different. No sooner had God miraculously rescued them from Egypt than the Israelites got distracted by their hardships.

READ & REFLECT

Read Exodus 16:1-4

- What were the Israelites distracted by?

- How did that affect their mood? Their faith? Their behavior?

There are scholars who believe that the journey from Egypt, where the Israelites were freed, to the Promised Land could have taken days, weeks, maybe a month or so. But because they kept getting distracted from God's faithfulness—over and over and over—they wandered that desert for forty years before God felt they were ready to enter their new home.

You see, we want to get to our destination as quickly as possible, but God cares about the journey. Of course, he also cares for the destination. God has a plan and purpose for your life—but he cares more about conforming you into the image of Jesus. This is our sanctification—our process of becoming like Jesus.

In *The Screwtape Letters* by C. S. Lewis, Screwtape, an experienced demon, writes letters to his nephew Wormwood, the new demon on the block doing his best to tempt a human from following Jesus. In one of the letters, Screwtape makes clear that distraction is a powerful tool for demons: "You can make him waste his time not only in conversations he enjoys with people whom he likes but also in conversations with those he cares nothing about, on subjects that bore him. You can make him do nothing at all for long periods. You can keep him up late at night, not roistering, but staring at a dead fire in a cold room."

- How has Satan used distraction as a temptation to keep you from following Jesus?

- What was the distraction? How did you find your way back? Are you still trying to find your way back?

Here is the inescapable and sometimes maddening truth: The wilderness is a place where God transforms us. Part of that transformation is teaching us to resist the distracting temptations that draw us away from God.

PRAY

As you complete your time of study today, pray about the distraction keeping you from following Jesus, and ask God to help you recognize it when it happens and resist it.

DAY 2

After God brings the Israelites out of Egypt and through the Red Sea, he settles them into their wilderness life. There he begins forming them into a great nation with laws and customs and festivals. He establishes his kingdom of priests and his holy nation (Exodus 19:6).

The Israelites have been worshiping God at Mount Sinai, and now it's time to continue the journey. Numbers 10:33-36 describes the presence of God leading the Israelites in the wilderness:

> They set out from the mountain of the LORD on a three-day journey with the ark of the LORD's covenant traveling ahead of

them for those three days to seek a resting place for them. Meanwhile, the cloud of the LORD was over them by day when they set out from the camp.

Whenever the ark set out, Moses would say:

Arise, LORD!
  Let your enemies be scattered,
  and those who hate you flee from your presence.

When it came to rest, he would say:

  Return, LORD,
  to the countless thousands of Israel.

But then something changes. Even though the Israelites have witnessed the ten plagues, the parting of the Red Sea, Moses' glowing face after meeting God at Mount Sinai, and Moses coming down the mountain carrying God's law, those memories fade when the going gets tough. Again and again, the Lord declares that they have no faith. Ouch.

Over and over, Israel gets distracted, forgets God's faithfulness, and openly rebels against him. Two of those occasions in Numbers are great examples of the problem.

READ & REFLECT

Read Numbers 11:1-20 and 12:1-15

For each story, answer the following:

- What was distracting people from God and God's purposes?

- What negative consequences did God give people?

- How did God provide for the people?

It can be disheartening to read about each of the times the people grumbled against God and rebelled against Moses. Despite their unfaithfulness, however, God shows himself faithful. Even his consequences are a sign of his faithfulness, using them to shape the Israelites into a people ready to enter the Promised Land.

These stories remind me of a quote I heard once by former Wheaton College president V. Raymond Edman: "Never doubt in the dark what God told you in the light." The Israelites questioned God; they questioned whether he would come through on his promise; they questioned whether Moses was the man for the job.

But why don't we have to question God? Again, we return to the truth of who God is—God's character. We can look to Scripture to see this. Let's mine the Psalms together.

In each of the verses below, circle or underline the words that describe God's characteristics:

> But you, Lord, are a compassionate and gracious God,
> slow to anger and abounding in faithful love and truth.
> (Psalm 86:15)

> The Lord is gracious and righteous;
> our God is compassionate. (Psalm 116:5)

> God our refuge and strength,
> a helper who is always found
> in times of trouble. (Psalm 46:1)

> God in his holy dwelling is
> a father of the fatherless
> and a champion of widows.

> God provides homes for those who are deserted.
> He leads out the prisoners to prosperity,
> but the rebellious live in a scorched land. (Psalm 68:5-6)

- With the descriptions of God that you have identified in these verses, think about this: How have you seen God show up in your life in these ways?

In many ways, the stories we read in Numbers show us how we are also likely to forget God's character. These stories highlight how fickle the human heart can be. Lest we get high and mighty, how often have we been found with no faith?

Thankfully, the whole point of the story of Scripture is not how great the Israelites are, or how great we are for that matter. It's how God is faithful to accomplish his covenant promise to Abraham, to bring all the nations into his family. God's fulfillment of his promise isn't dependent on our faithfulness but his.

PRAY

As you close your time today in prayer, consider praying these words of the psalmist:

> Blessed be the Lord!
> Day after day he bears our burdens;
> God is our salvation. *Selah*
> Our God is a God of salvation. (Psalm 68:19-20)

DAY 3

In the book of Numbers, we see all the hardships the Israelites go through, and they are legitimate hardships! They may not be enslaved anymore, but they are circling around a desert with little food and water, unsure of when they will reach their destination. And then, just when they are about to enter the Promised Land, they learn that there are powerful enemies in the land who will try to stop them from entering.

READ & REFLECT

Read Numbers 13:26-33

- How are the Israelites being distracted from the promises of God?

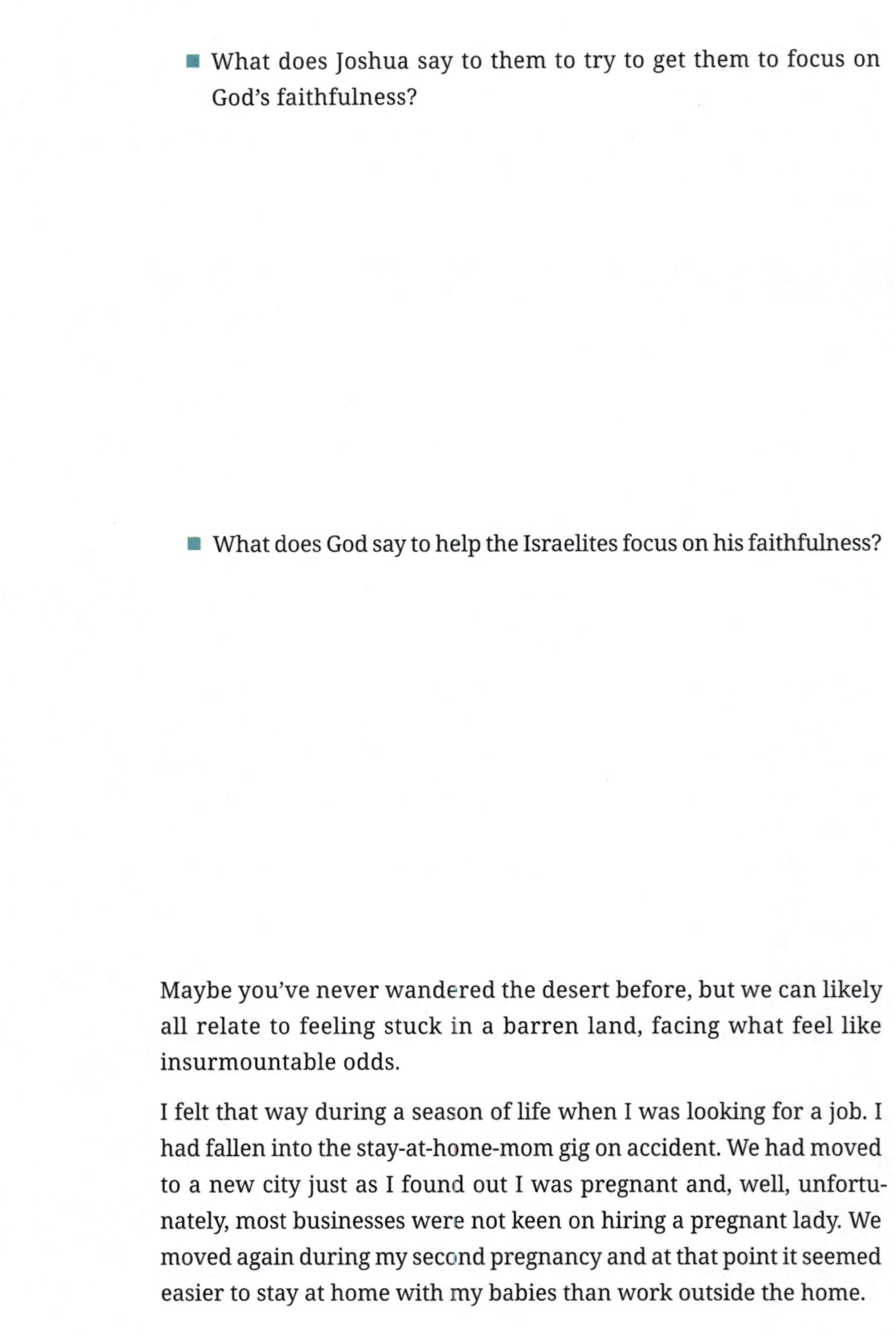

- What does Joshua say to them to try to get them to focus on God's faithfulness?

- What does God say to help the Israelites focus on his faithfulness?

Maybe you've never wandered the desert before, but we can likely all relate to feeling stuck in a barren land, facing what feel like insurmountable odds.

I felt that way during a season of life when I was looking for a job. I had fallen into the stay-at-home-mom gig on accident. We had moved to a new city just as I found out I was pregnant and, well, unfortunately, most businesses were not keen on hiring a pregnant lady. We moved again during my second pregnancy and at that point it seemed easier to stay at home with my babies than work outside the home.

After a while, finances were tight! I knew I needed to find a job where I could contribute financially, but all I heard were rejections or crickets. I felt at the end of my rope wondering why God had forgotten me and my family. I worked a lot of odd jobs with seemingly no direction and no prospects for growth. The debt grew and my husband and I felt despair. How would we get out of this? How would we provide for our young family?

Jesus said, "In this world you will have trouble." Sounds bleak! But let's read the verse in full: "I have told you these things, so that in me you may have peace. In this world you will have trouble. But take heart! I have overcome the world" (John 16:33 NIV).

- What reason does Jesus give for us to have peace in the midst of trouble?

- Have you ever experienced peace during times of trouble? What was that like?

Sometimes when we go through difficult times, our circumstances can distract us from who God is and what God has promised. In their own time of trouble, the Israelites chose grumbling. Fortunately for them (and for us!), our God is not changed by our thoughts, feelings, or behaviors. He is faithful, even when we are faithless (2 Timothy 2:13).

I'll admit I didn't have a lot of faith in the season I described above. I felt angry and abandoned. I took my eyes off of Jesus and set them squarely on our pile of bills and my unused seminary degree collecting dust in a closet. But little by little, God began to show himself faithful. His provision didn't always look like how I wanted it to look (I found a part-time job eventually . . . as an accountant at a small freight company . . . and let me tell you, this writer does not do math), but he did provide. I remember having a hard conversation one day that involved a very hard no and walking out feeling at peace because I knew it wasn't the end of the story. God had more for our family even if I didn't know what it was yet. The same is true for you. If you're still breathing, God's not done. There's more.

PRAY

Loving Father, we know that you are always with us. Although we are promised suffering in this world, we are also promised your presence. When we are tempted to grumble, when we become distracted, help us to hold on to the truth that you are always with us. Let us not long to return to Egypt, to the shackles of sin, but to press on and choose you. In Jesus' name, amen.

DAY 4

I can't help but believe that the greatest temptation the Israelites faced and succumbed to was making themselves the center of the story. It's what happened to Adam and Eve. It's a temptation we all feel. We want to place ourselves at the center of the story with main character energy—*our* pain, *our* hurts, *our* desires, *our* plans. But this is God's story. While it is true that God loves and values us; while it is true that

God has a magnificent plan for our lives—it is God who is at the center, and it is we who orbit around him. He created us and made us in his image, not the other way around.

Just as God used the wilderness to transform Israel, God can use the wilderness to transform you into someone who can focus on God—on God's goodness, holiness, and faithfulness.

READ & REFLECT

Read James 1:2-16

- List everything that can distract us from our faith in God. (Hint: Nearly every verse contains a possible distraction.)

- List all of the benefits that can come from trials and temptations if we persevere.

Satan can use the wilderness to distract us. But for those of us who persevere, God uses the wilderness to help us grow spiritually strong—not as a punishment, but as refinement. As a way to shed distractions and focus intently on God and the person he is forming us to be. We can even rejoice in our afflictions, because through these trials, we are made mature in our faith.

Now, I don't want you to walk away from today's study thinking you cannot be honest about your pain. Hebrews 4:16 says we can approach God's throne with confidence to receive grace and mercy. We can be our full and honest selves to God. We do this, however, remembering that God is faithful, God is wise, God has a plan, God is hope. We walk in the wilderness expectantly, knowing God will act.

Still, persevering is not easy. How do we keep our eyes focused on God in the midst of trials and temptations?

Read Numbers 21:6-8

- What trial were the Israelites going through?

- What did God tell the people to focus on in order to be saved?

Read John 3:13-15

- How does Jesus compare himself to the snake on Moses' pole?

- What does Jesus tell the people to do in order to be saved?

In the midst of an infestation of venomous snakes, it must have been hard for the Israelites to remember God's promises. But those who took their eyes off of themselves and the serpents all around to look up at God's means of forgiveness and grace were saved. Jesus references this very story when telling his listeners he would need to die and be lifted up on the cross just as the snake was lifted up on the pole. To those who knew the story of the Israelites in the desert, and to those who would remember Jesus' comparison after his death, John 3 is Jesus' invitation to keep our eyes on the cross.

The cross is one of the most distinct symbols of the Christian faith. As a child, my family attended mass at our neighborhood Catholic church. Behind the altar was a crucifix. I remember wondering how this could be an adored symbol. How could this be a picture of God's love and faithfulness?

To the world, the cross is foolish. Crucifixion was nothing to be celebrated in ancient times. Hanging on a cross was degrading. It meant you were a criminal. It meant you were subhuman, shamed, and tortured. It meant God had forgotten you.

But God's kingdom is an upside-down kingdom and the cross is where God begins to make all things new. When we look at the cross, we see God's love, hope, joy, and peace. As Christ-followers we can look at the cross as a tangible reminder of God's fulfilled promise.

- How has the cross as a symbol helped you persevere through the wilderness without getting distracted? (If the cross has not been that for you, how might you reconsider the meaning of the cross?)

- Are there ways you could use a physical cross—in the form of a holding cross or necklace pendant, for instance—to help you focus on God's goodness, forgiveness, and faithfulness?

PRAY

As you end your time of study today, pray the prayer below as a reminder of God's faithfulness:

God, you are always faithful. You have always shown yourself to be faithful. From freeing the Israelites from slavery to providing manna in the wilderness to giving your Son, Jesus, so that we would be with you forever. When I begin to doubt, help me to look back at the cross and empty tomb as reminders of your faithfulness. In Jesus' name, amen.

DAY 5

REFLECTION DAY

Centering Prayer

Hopefully throughout this week you have had an opportunity to reflect on who God is, his faithfulness, and his goodness. And hopefully you will feel a nudge to focus on Jesus and the cross when you are being distracted by the cares of the world.

Whenever I'm not sure what to read in the Bible I turn to the Psalms. I love the versatility of the Psalms. You can find psalms for almost any occasion—when you're overjoyed, when you're anxious, when you're grieved, when you're thankful.

Psalm 106 recalls the story of the Israelites in the wilderness in poetic form. It's honest and raw about what the Israelites did and the hardships they endured. But it's even more honest about who God is and recognizes the praise due God's name. It's a beautiful model of growing strong spiritually by acknowledging hardships without letting them distract you from God's goodness and faithfulness.

Read Psalm 106

After reading the psalm, I want you to try centering prayer. This is a form of Christian contemplative prayer, a method of silent prayer that seeks to eliminate outside distractions so we can focus on Jesus and experience God's presence. Some people practice centering prayer for twenty minutes, but if it's your first time, I suggest picking an amount of time that sounds reasonable to you.

1. Sit comfortably with your eyes closed. Relax, be still, and know God is with you.
2. Choose a sacred word to focus on. You may want to choose a word from Psalm 106, which you just read. Sacred words are not used as mantras, as in constantly repeating them, but as a reminder of your intention to remain open.
3. When distractions come to mind, be gentle with yourself. Set the distraction aside by saying the sacred word you chose. Think of it as a reset button.
4. After your allotted time, you can open your eyes, thank God for your time together, and go about your day.

Don't spend time worrying if you "did it right." Just let it be. If you choose to continue practicing centering prayer, it will become more natural to you and you may be able to extend the time in which you engage in this type of prayer.

WEEK 5

THE WILDERNESS OF DESPAIR

Group Session

All of us, at one point or another, experience despair—the feeling of hopelessness that can come with tough seasons. For some of us this can spiral into depression or other mental health challenges. But even if it doesn't, it can be difficult to navigate these feelings. This week we will talk about what it's like when feelings of despair seem to overtake us and how God meets us there.

VIDEO

Watch this week's video. 

OPENING ACTIVITY

In the video I shared how difficult it was for me to identify and then tell people I was feeling depressed. I'm not alone in having difficulty identifying the ways I am struggling. In fact, researcher Brené Brown reports in *Atlas of the Heart* that participants could reliably identify only three emotions as they were experiencing them: happiness, sadness, and anger. But God made us to experience a full range of emotions, and it's helpful to practice naming them. Look through the list below and circle four or five words that best capture moments when you feel low:

humiliated	ashamed	vulnerable
numb	hopeless	disconnected
lost	despairing	depressed
alienated	forlorn	disappointed
exhausted	disheartened	discouraged
burned out	helpless	tired
lonely	frightened	miserable

Share your words with the group. If you'd like, take one minute to share what circumstances are most likely to elicit these emotions.

1. When you feel these emotions, do you feel like you can talk to God about it? Why or why not?

REFLECT

Read 1 Kings 17:1-16

Elijah is originally from Gilead, a fertile region given to the Israelites as part of the Promised Land. After Elijah prophesies a drought to the powerful Israelite king in verse 1, God sends him to the Kerith Ravine. *Kerith* means "cutting" or "separation."

2. How do verses 2-6 describe Elijah's life in the Kerith Ravine?

3. Compared to his life in Gilead, how is the ravine a wilderness to Elijah? From what has he been separated?

When the water runs dry, God sends Elijah to meet a widow who is in a desperate situation.

4. How is the widow's situation similar to Elijah's?

5. How is her outlook on her situation different from Elijah's?

6. Summarize God's encouragement to the widow, spoken through Elijah, in verses 13-14.

7. In what ways does God allow Elijah and the widow to minister to one another in their time of desperation?

8. How do both Elijah and the widow have to admit their vulnerability and need in order for them to receive help?

9. When you are feeling despair (or in a desperate situation), are you more likely to respond like Elijah or the widow? How?

Take a couple of minutes to read the text silently.

10. How is this passage an encouragement to you when you feel despair?

11. How is this passage an encouragement to you as you minister to those in the wilderness of despair?

PRAY

Lord God, you are so good to meet us where we are. We have the honor of coming before you just as we are. We can be honest about our struggles and we know you will love us in the midst of it. You also are good to give us people, a family, where we can encourage one another and walk together through life's hardships. When we feel the temptation to turn inward, help us to reach out through the power of your Spirit. We are grateful. In Jesus' name, amen.

If time allows, share with one another any prayer requests and bring them to our faithful and trustworthy God in prayer.

DAY 1

After three years, Elijah goes looking for King Ahab again. This time Elijah goes up against 450 prophets of Baal, whom Ahab and many of the Israelites had been worshiping. Elijah is victorious and Ahab's wife Jezebel is enraged.

READ & REFLECT

Read 1 Kings 19:1-5

- Why does Elijah end up in the wilderness?

- How does he respond—emotionally and behaviorally—to Jezebel's threat?

- How is this response different from his response in chapter 17, when he ran out of water and food?

My son has always had big feelings. In early motherhood I felt overwhelmed, unsure of how to handle these feelings, and I often allowed his mood to direct my mood. Over the years I've learned how to help him navigate his big feelings—how to name them, regulate them, and express them without shame.

Growing up, there was an expectation in our family that I would be emotionally "neutral." I too was a child with big feelings—often throwing tantrums as a toddler. But I learned that these displays of emotions were unacceptable. I remember being told to stop crying, settle down, cut it out.

But what happens when we hold everything in? Our feelings often turn into anxiety and depression, and we end up breaking down. That's what happened to me off and on for years.

So I appreciate Elijah's honesty in these verses. He's not trying to put on a brave face. He's not trying to see the silver lining. He is alone in the wilderness, tired and worn out. He is done, similar to the widow in chapter 17. Unlike the widow, though, Elijah takes his despair to the Lord. He tells God about his pain and hopelessness.

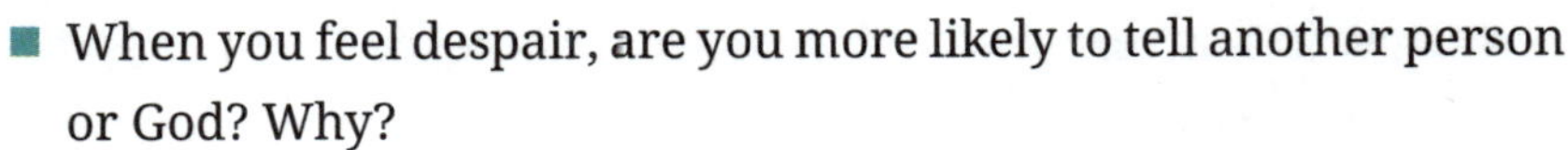

- When you feel despair, are you more likely to tell another person or God? Why?

- How do you hope they will respond?

Sometimes when we are sad, we receive unhelpful advice. Over the years I've been told to snap out of it, think happy thoughts, or "just stop." But God doesn't tell us any of those things.

Read 1 Peter 5:6-11

- How do these verses affirm Elijah for crying out, "I have had enough, Lord?"

- In what ways might these verses have encouraged Elijah if they had been available when he was alive?

- In what ways do these verses encourage you?

PRAY

End your time today by completing the following prayer based on 1 Kings 19 and 1 Peter 5.

Lord, my adversary the devil prowls around like a roaring lion, seeking to devour. I have had enough and I am casting my cares on you:

I am firm in my faith, knowing that my brothers and sisters throughout the world are experiencing the same kinds of suffering. I thank you ahead of time that after I have suffered a little while, you, who have called me to eternal glory in Christ, will restore, confirm, strengthen, and establish me. To you be the power forever and ever. Amen.

DAY 2

READ & REFLECT

Read 1 Kings 19:4-9

- After Elijah expresses a desire to die, how does God restore his vitality?

- What must Elijah do to cooperate with God during this time?

- Why do you think the author of 1 Kings included the detail that Elijah went to sleep three separate times in just five verses?

"Get up and eat, for the journey is too much for you" (1 Kings 19:7 NIV). That line is so tender. The voice in my head as I read this is that of a loving parent nursing a child back to health. And all Elijah had to do in response was willingly receive the nourishment provided and rest.

He didn't have to muster up his energy to keep going. He didn't have to prove that he was still faithful. He simply had to willingly *receive* and *rest*. Let's return again to our definition of spiritual strength: reliance on and alignment with the Holy Spirit, a resilience that develops when we trust God to do the work in and through us. In the wilderness of despair, growing in spiritual strength looks like receiving nourishment and rest.

There's something powerful about meals. One of the ways my abuelita says "I love you" is by serving up a hot plate of gallo pinto (Nicaraguan red beans and rice) and tortillas. It's not fancy, but it's delicious and nourishing. My abuelita and I lived together from the time I was nine years old until I got married. During those years I experienced many ups and downs. From failing a math test to getting my heart broken to graduating high school to bringing home my now husband to meet her for the first time. And gallo pinto was almost always on the stove. It's a comforting reminder of her love.

- Think of a favorite comfort food. What's the positive association you have with that food? How does it make you feel?

I imagine this is what Elijah felt when he saw the loaf of warm bread and jug of water God had provided for him. He might have been surprised to see this food in the middle of the wilderness, but then again, maybe he wasn't. After all, he knew that God is Jehovah-Jireh (or Yahweh-Yireh)—the God who provides. All he needed to do was receive.

When Elijah was running away from God, God was running after Elijah. But God wasn't running after Elijah to scold him. God ran after Elijah to nourish him and then to give him time to rest some more.

Read Matthew 11:28-30

- How does Jesus describe the rest he provides?

Some people hear the word *rest* and breathe a sigh of relief. Others hear that word and immediately feel anxious and guilty. *There's no time to rest! There's too much to do! I haven't earned it!*

- How do you respond to Jesus' invitation to give you rest? What's your default?

When despair hits it's important to be soft with ourselves and take time to rest. It's important to acknowledge our feelings and express them. It is equally important not to stay in that place.

As I shared earlier, I'm an introvert who has no problem being alone. When I go through hard times, I tend to turn inward. My bed is my best friend and I shut the world out. And that may be necessary to do for a time, but I also need to resolve to get up.

God's kindness allowed Elijah to rest, and that same kindness helped Elijah get up again—first to eat the food God offered and then to re-engage with his mission as a prophet, walking forty days to Mount Horeb.

- Has there been a time when God has provided something for you when you were ready to give up? Was it in the form of nourishment, rest, or encouragement to get up? Something else?

- How did God's provisions change things for you?

PRAY

Take a few minutes to end your study today by writing a prayer to God. Ask the Holy Spirit to guide you in seeing God's provision in your life.

DAY 3

READ & REFLECT

Read 1 Kings 19:10-12

- How does Elijah respond when asked why he is in the cave?

- Name at least four emotions you hear in Elijah's response to the Lord in verse 10. (If you need ideas, refer back to the list of emotions found in this week's group study.)

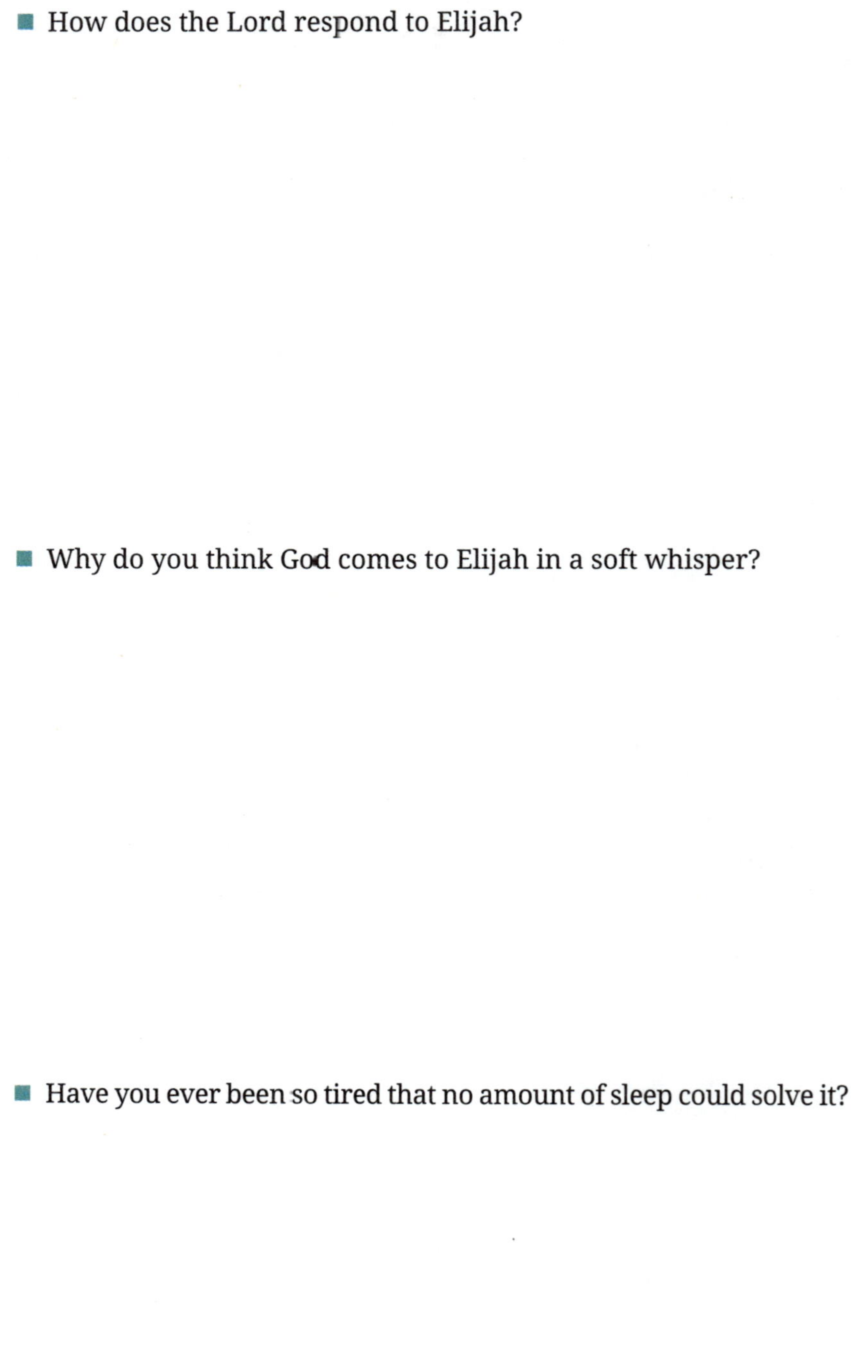

- How does the Lord respond to Elijah?

- Why do you think God comes to Elijah in a soft whisper?

- Have you ever been so tired that no amount of sleep could solve it?

Dr. Saundra Dalton-Smith is a mental health professional who talks about rest. I came to know her because she regularly teaches at our church about mental health and the importance of rest in our lives. In one message, she talked about the seven types of rest she writes about in her book *Sacred Rest*: mental, emotional, social, sensory, creative, and physical. As she spoke about these different types of rest, something clicked in my mind—the type of tired I was feeling couldn't be solved with a nap.

I wasn't physically tired; *I was soul tired.*

Earlier in 1 Kings 19, God dealt with Elijah's need for physical rest—God allowed Elijah to sleep and provided nourishment for him. But now it was time to deal with Elijah's need for spiritual rest.

One way we become spiritually tired, according to Dr. Dalton-Smith, is trying to perform for God rather than spending time in relationship with God. Spending time in God's presence is necessary for all believers. Life in our modern-day reality is noisy, busy, and fast-paced. We must learn how to turn down the volume of life so we can turn up the volume of God's voice.

In her book *Invitation to Solitude and Silence*, Ruth Haley Barton says, "Because we do not rest, we lose our way. . . . Poisoned by the hypnotic belief that good things come only through unceasing determination and tireless effort, we can never truly rest. And for want of rest our lives are in danger."

- In what ways do you try to perform for God?

- What gets in the way of hearing God's voice?

- What would it look like for you to create space regularly to listen to God's voice?

Today's study is not meant to induce guilt. We all get busy. We all have responsibilities. But if we truly want rest and if we truly want to hear from God, we must learn to make space.

When I was a young mom, spending time with God often felt impossible. I had my babies back-to-back and neither one of them liked to sleep. I was up at all hours rocking a toddler or feeding a baby or changing a diaper. One place my kids always napped was in the car, so most days after lunch time, I would strap them into their car seats and drive around the neighborhood until they were fast asleep. Then I would get myself a chai latte from the Starbucks drive-through and sit in our driveway.

As I sat and rested from the demands of motherhood with my overpriced drink, I would pull out my phone and read a devotional from my Bible app. That was the extent of my Bible study at the time—a few stolen minutes in the middle of the day as my babies slept soundly in their car seats. There were no commentaries, no highlighters, no grand *aha* moments—just a tired mom desperate for a word from the Lord. And you know what? God met me there.

No matter our personalities or seasons of life, we all need time in God's presence. We can let life get in the way, or we can fight for that time and protect it fiercely. Silence and solitude are important components of spending time in God's presence. This is not the only place we find God. All of life is worship and we can commune with God at any time, but I am convinced that "being still," as is stipulated throughout Scripture, is necessary for our spiritual health. Again, Ruth Haley Barton puts it this way: "We are starved for quiet, to hear the sound of sheer silence that is the presence of God himself."

Read Psalm 46

- What are all of the circumstances that could lead to despair?

- In the midst of these desperate circumstances, God is a refuge and strength. How else does the psalmist describe God?

- Based on verses 8 and 10, what actions can we take in order to experience God's goodness and power?

PRAY

To end your study time today, choose one of the verses from Psalm 46 to focus on as you sit in silence for a few minutes. Allow the words to wash over you. Listen for God's voice. Don't be discouraged if you don't "hear" anything right away. Being still is a practice and learning to recognize God's voice takes time. The more we practice and the more we meditate on God's Word (the Bible), the more we will recognize God's voice in the soft whisper.

DAY 4

READ & REFLECT

Read 1 Kings 19:9-14

- Verses 9-10 are virtually identical to verses 13-14. Why might we have expected Elijah's response in 14 to be different from his response in 10?

I love Elijah's honesty. He has the audacity to tell God exactly what's going on and exactly how he's feeling. I'm especially moved by his honesty in verse 14. His lament has not changed by even one word—even after the word of the Lord graciously guides him to the mouth of the cave where he can be in God's presence, even after he connects with him through the gentle whisper. He is weary and doesn't see that anything has changed. He is still stuck in a cave, hiding from those who want to kill him, and that's what he tells God.

I didn't grow up thinking I could be this honest with God. When you think about it, that's kind of silly. Doesn't God already know what I'm thinking anyway? But I didn't want to seem ungrateful; after all, other people had it way worse. But God invites us to share with him, even when it's the same old lament. Even when God has been gracious to us and our faith "should" be stronger. God wants us to share.

Now that Elijah has shared how he felt that he was all alone, God responds with a loving solution: community.

Read 1 Kings 19:15-21

- How does God show Elijah that he is not alone?

- How does Elisha respond to Elijah in verses 20-21? What does that tell you about Elisha?

- At the end of this chapter, if God had asked once again, "What are you doing here, Elijah?" how do you think he would have responded?

What I like about this part of the story is that God helped Elijah see he wasn't alone. There were at least seven thousand others who remained faithful to God. When Elijah was on the brink of despair and ready to give up due to the lonely calling of serving Yahweh, God told him to get up and anoint two kings to help rid Israel of idol worship and to anoint Elisha as his successor.

Whenever I enter a depressive episode, I tend to turn inward. I think this is common for most people. I become focused on my problems and start to believe the lie that I am all alone in the world. I have a hard time opening up to anyone and think I have to deal with it on my own.

The truth is that we are created for community because we are made in the image and likeness of the one true God, who is love and who has existed in an eternal community of self-giving love. God is one being that externally exists in three coequal, coeternal persons—Father, Son, and Spirit. Since we are made in God's image, we too are created to live in loving community. We may think intimacy with God is all that we need, but it wasn't enough for Elijah, and it's not enough for us.

Spiritual strength means relying on God, but it doesn't mean going it alone, just you and God. Sometimes spiritual strength means receiving the community God sends you in the wilderness.

- How have you been blessed by community?

- What has made connecting in community difficult at times?

When I moved with my family to South Carolina, I decided I would serve in our church's teens ministry. As a thirty-something, I knew I had something to offer the younger women at our church. So each week I have showed up to lead this group, to teach them what I know about following Jesus, to listen to their perspectives, and to learn from them. There have been weeks when I didn't necessarily feel like showing up, but I honored my commitment and, in turn, I was able to gain perspective. When I started feeling down about the state of our world, or even just the state of my own life, being with these girls week in and week out helped me look outside of myself to see the bigger picture.

Maybe your calling isn't necessarily to lead a group of teens, and that's okay! How can you intentionally connect to community? It could be that this group you're currently meeting with is it. Walking through this study together doesn't have to be just an exercise in biblical study—this can be a space where you commit to sharing your lives together, encouraging one another, and reminding each other of the bigger picture.

Elijah and Elisha go on to have a fruitful ministry. While the Bible doesn't give us many details, we presume Elijah mentors Elisha until it's time for Elisha to step out on his own. Likewise, Elisha has a hand in helping Elijah out of his despair (whether he realizes it or not). We can do the same for others and others can do the same for us.

- Who is someone in your life who mentored you? How did that relationship change you?

- Who might God be calling you to mentor?

- How might mentoring another person alleviate despair or re-ignite your faith?

PRAY

As you end your study today, pray about an encouraging Bible verse you can text to a friend. In this way you will be connecting to God's Word and connecting to a person in a simple but meaningful way.

DAY 5

REFLECTION DAY

Breath Prayer (Psalm 6)

Breathe in, breathe out. This has not been an easy week. We talked about difficult topics, but I hope one message rang true: When you experience the wilderness of despair, you can develop spiritual strength by receiving God's gifts of rest, nourishment, and community. Elijah received those gifts, and so can you.

Let's try a breath prayer for our reflection day. Calling attention to our breathing is helpful for regulation and relaxation. It supports our movement, our mental state, and our endurance. Most breath prayers are six to eight syllables and fit easily into one inhale and exhale. You can use a Bible verse or make up your own refrain.

Here are some instructions to prepare you for a breath prayer, as well as a few prompts.

1. Sit comfortably, close your eyes, and remember that God loves you and you are in God's presence.
2. Imagine God calling you by name, as he did with Elijah in 1 Kings 19:9, asking you, "What are you doing here, [Your Name]?"
3. Answer God honestly with whatever word or phrase comes from deep within you.
4. Use the Scriptures below (adapted from Psalm 6) as you inhale and exhale.
5. Remember that God's kindness will meet you and his presence will be a sweet reward. I am praying in advance that you will hear God's voice and feel his arms wrap around you. You're home.

Inhale: Be gracious to me, Lord.

Exhale: For I am weak.

Inhale: Turn, Lord, rescue me.

Exhale: Save me with your faithful love.

Inhale: The Lord has heard my plea.

Exhale: The Lord accepts my prayer.

Repeat as many times as you like.

WEEK 6

THE WILDERNESS OF TEMPTATION

Group Session

Even Jesus experienced the wilderness in his lifetime. The beautiful thing about his wilderness experience is that he shows us a way through it. In Jesus we see the important role of Scripture in our lives. The Bible is a "light to our path" through the wilderness and is accessible to us all.

VIDEO

Watch this week's video. 

OPENING ACTIVITY

One of the ways God strengthens us is with his Word. Take a moment to share something about your relationship with the Bible.

1. What were you taught about the Bible growing up?

2. How has the Bible shaped you today? (If this study was your first time reading Scripture, what was that like?)

Studying the Bible in a group is a great way to grow in your faith!

3. How has reading the Bible together in this group been helpful to you?

REFLECT

Read Matthew 4:1-11

4. Who leads Jesus into the wilderness? Why?

5. What is significant about Jesus fasting for forty days? (Hint: Where else in the Bible have we seen people in the wilderness for forty days or nights? We've studied two of those instances in this book already!)

6. What are the three ways Jesus is tempted? If you had to give each temptation a one-word name, what would those words be?

7. How do these three temptations show up in your own life?

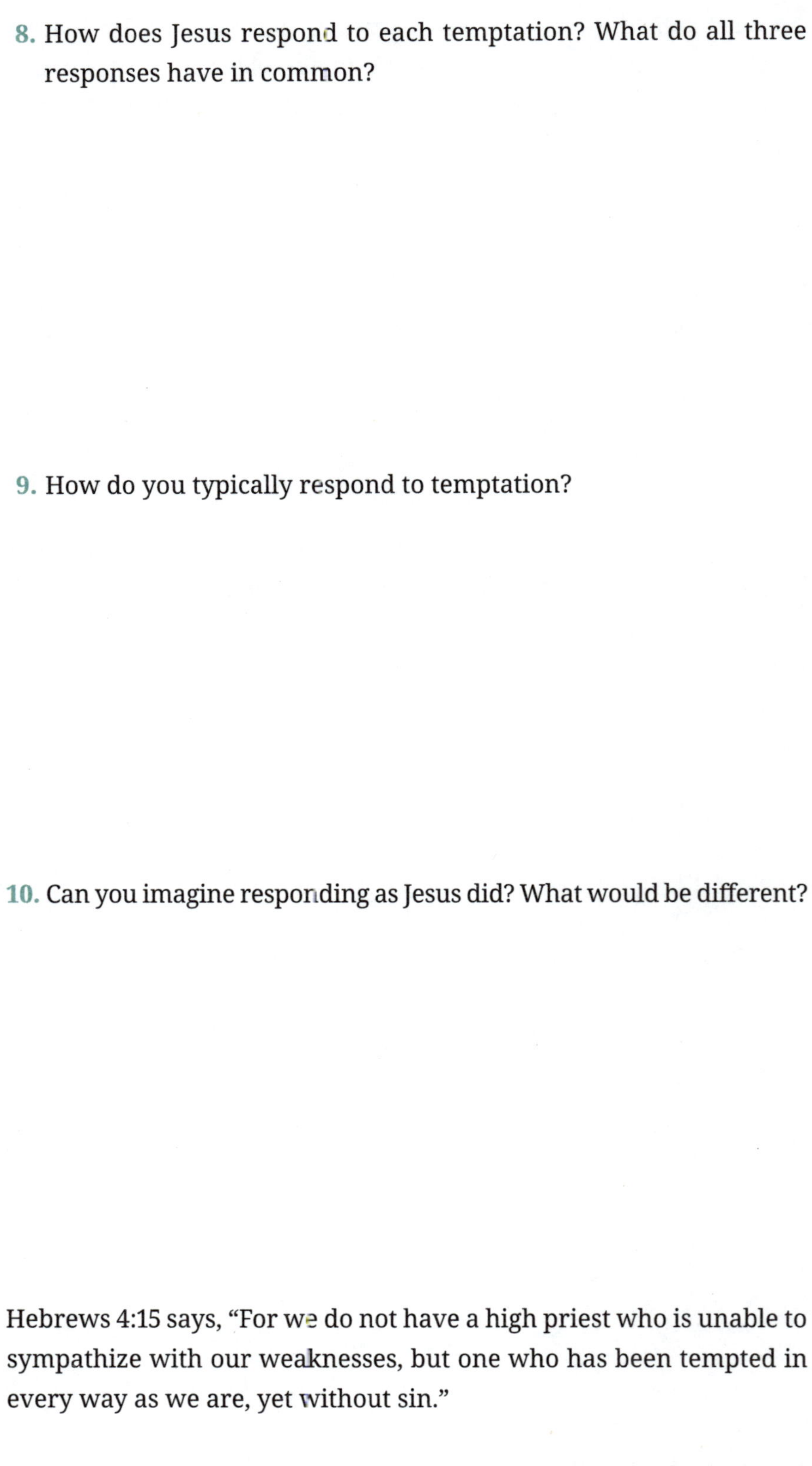

8. How does Jesus respond to each temptation? What do all three responses have in common?

9. How do you typically respond to temptation?

10. Can you imagine responding as Jesus did? What would be different?

Hebrews 4:15 says, "For we do not have a high priest who is unable to sympathize with our weaknesses, but one who has been tempted in every way as we are, yet without sin."

11. How do this passage and Jesus' experience in the wilderness encourage you when you are facing temptation?

12. How can they help you think about times of wilderness or temptation as opportunities to be formed in the likeness of Christ?

PRAY

Father, Son, and Spirit, we come before you to express our gratitude for providing this space where we can wrestle with what the wilderness is and how it forms us in your image. We thank you that the hardships we endure are not in vain and that you have given us your Spirit and your Word to guide us and show us a way through the wilderness. In Jesus' name, amen.

If time allows, share with one another any prayer requests and bring them to our faithful and trustworthy God in prayer.

DAY 1

Before going into the wilderness, Jesus did something profound that can help us as we think about our own wilderness experiences.

READ & REFLECT

Read Matthew 3:13-17

- What was John's logic for not baptizing Jesus?

- How did Jesus convince John to baptize him?

- People have described verses 16 and 17 as a coronation of sorts, an anointing of a king. What elements of this scene share elements with a coronation?

Have you ever wondered why Jesus got baptized? After all, John's baptism was one of repentance. He called people to the waters of the Jordan so they could be cleansed from their sins. But Jesus didn't have sin. So what was the purpose of his baptism? There could be several reasons:

- He wanted to be an example for future believers to follow.
- He wanted to identify with us and our need.
- It was a symbol of his redemptive work.
- This was prophetic of his death, burial, and resurrection.

Whatever the reason, Jesus said it was to "fulfill all righteousness." I love that—although he had no need to be cleansed from sin, he entered the waters of baptism to fulfill all righteousness. When the dove came down over him and God declared him a beloved son, Jesus was stamped "approved" for all to see.

Let's read the words God told Jesus one more time: "This is my beloved Son, with whom I am well-pleased."

As mentioned before, this baptism takes place before Jesus enters his public ministry. He hasn't really done anything yet, so why is God well-pleased with him?

I come from an immigrant family. My parents are some of the most supportive people you'll ever meet. I have never lacked their love and acceptance. But there is a certain pressure that comes from being in an immigrant family. My parents risked it all to escape a war-torn country and come to the United States, a place where they didn't speak the language and had no guaranteed jobs. They came with hopes of freedom and success not only for themselves but for their daughters.

I didn't want to waste the opportunity for which they had risked their lives. And so I wanted to perform to the best of my ability—but no matter how good you are at what you do, failures will come, exhaustion will come, burnout will come. Trying to perform at all times is crippling. We get stuck in our cycles of performance. We buy into the lie that if we perform well, we will gain the approval we so desperately want.

In the story of Jesus' baptism we see that he did not have to perform in order to gain the approval of his Father. Neither do we.

You can rest from your performance. You don't have to work for approval; you are already approved. Yes, God can use the wilderness to help you grow spiritually strong, but you don't have to perform your way out of it. God's love and approval are the foundation of our spiritual strength, and they are yours, before you enter the wilderness, in the wilderness, and when you leave the wilderness.

- Is seeking approval something you struggle with? How has it affected your life?

- What might change if you believed God was saying, "You are my beloved child, with whom I am well-pleased"?

PRAY

As God is forming you into the likeness of Christ, remain faithful that he can and will carry you through and that his love for and approval of you are steadfast. As you close your study time today, write a prayer of gratitude to God for the love and approval that are already yours in Christ. You might want to base it on Psalm 139:13-15 (NIV):

> For you created my inmost being;
> you knit me together in my mother's womb.
> I praise you because I am fearfully and wonderfully made;
> your works are wonderful,
> I know that full well.
> My frame was not hidden from you
> when I was made in the secret place,
> when I was woven together in the depths of the earth.

DAY 2

Jesus faces temptation in the wilderness. There is something about this temptation experience that further prepares him for ministry and his ultimate redemption of humanity. This is a necessary experience for Jesus. I would venture to say the wilderness is a necessary experience for us as well as we learn to face temptation like Jesus did—by using Scripture as a weapon. This is what Adam and Eve, and later Moses, failed to do. Let's compare their responses to temptation.

READ & REFLECT

Read Luke 4:1-13; Genesis 2:16-17; Genesis 3:1-6; and Numbers 20:2-12

Pay attention to what each character does with the Word of God, then fill in the following chart.

Original Word of God	How God's Word Is Used in the Face of Temptation
Man does not live on bread alone but on every word that comes from the mouth of the LORD. (Deuteronomy 8:3)	[Jesus] answered, "It is written: Man must not live on bread alone but on every word that comes from the mouth of God." (Matthew 4:4)
Fear the LORD your God, worship him, and take your oaths in his name. (Deuteronomy 6:13) Do not test the LORD your God as you tested him at Massah. (Deuteronomy 6:16)	"It is written: Worship the Lord your God, and serve only him." (Matthew 4:10) "It is also written: Do not test the Lord your God." (Matthew 4:7)
The LORD spoke to Moses, "Take the staff and assemble the community. You and your brother Aaron are to speak to the rock while they watch, and it will yield its water." (Numbers 20:7-8)	Moses raised his hand and struck the rock twice with his staff. (Numbers 20:11)
"You are free to eat from any tree of the garden, but you must not eat from the tree of the knowledge of good and evil, for on the day you eat from it, you will certainly die." (Genesis 2:16-17)	The woman said to the serpent, "We may eat the fruit from the trees in the garden. But about the fruit of the tree in the middle of the garden, God said, 'You must not eat it or touch it, or you will die.'" (Genesis 3:2-3)

Adam, Eve, Moses, and Jesus are all armed with the Word of God. Unfortunately, Adam, Eve, and Moses are spiritually weak—twisting God's word and taking matters into their own hands. Eve adds to God's command, making it stricter than God intended, and Satan uses that distortion to further tempt her to eat the fruit. Moses seemingly ignores God's command, and instead of speaking to the rock he strikes it.

Adam, Eve, and Moses are tested, and they all fail. As a result, Adam and Eve are cast out of the garden, and Moses is not allowed to enter the Promised Land after forty years of wandering the desert.

	How are they the same? Different?

You may remember that Jesus is in the wilderness for forty days. These numbers are not a coincidence. They are a clue to the reader that the stories are linked. In theology this is called "recapitulation."

All these stories are layered on top of each other. In their juxtaposition we see how God is preparing to do something beautiful. Jesus' trip into the wilderness is not in vain. God retells the story of Adam and Eve, who were meant to co-rule with God in the garden, and the story of Moses, who was meant to bring his people into the Promised Land, through Jesus.

Where Adam, Eve, and Moses fail, Jesus succeeds. Now in Christ, we join Jesus in our original purpose of being co-rulers meant to lead people into the kingdom of God.

- When you look at the three stories layered on top of each other, what stands out to you?

- What new commitments might you make to study and memorize the Word of God so that you will be spiritually strong when faced with temptation?

In the wilderness, Jesus reverses what occurred with Adam and Eve and with the Israelites, using God's Word as a weapon to fight temptation. Jesus retells the story of Adam and the story of Israel by going into the wilderness and being victorious in it. Through him, we too can be victorious in the wilderness.

PRAY

As you end your study today, meditate on this refrain found throughout the Psalms:

> Give thanks to the LORD, for he is good;
> his faithful love endures forever. (Psalm 118:29)

DAY 3

READ & REFLECT

Read Matthew 4:11-17

- Why do you think angels need to attend to Jesus in verse 13?

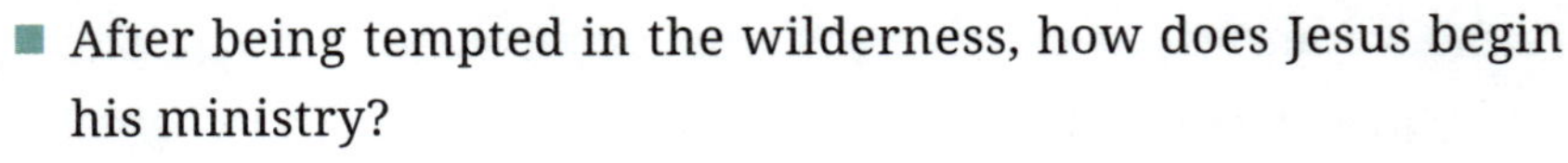

- After being tempted in the wilderness, how does Jesus begin his ministry?

- What is Jesus' primary message?

- What do you think it means that the "kingdom of heaven has come near"?

A noteworthy aspect of Jesus' time in the wilderness is that it comes after his baptism but before his public ministry begins. In these forty days of seclusion in the wilderness, he has the opportunity to train, meditate, and prepare for his ministry.

When I look back at my own life, I see how this has been my experience. When I graduated from seminary, I wanted to hit the ground running in ministry. I cleaned up my résumé and applied for job after job, only to be let down again and again. I entered a wilderness season that lasted for several years. In fact, I wouldn't get hired to work on a church staff until eight years after I graduated. (And finding steady work of any kind before then proved to be difficult.)

Since being hired to work on staff at my local church, ministry has been active indeed. I'm thankful for the eight years I had to grow strong in spirit. Years where God formed me more into the image of Jesus, whittled away arrogance, and prepared me for this current season of ministering, writing, and teaching.

- If you are currently in the wilderness, what might God be preparing you for?

- If you've exited the wilderness, how did God use that time to prepare you?

Whether you're wandering in the wilderness or sitting in the sanctuary now, take time to thank God for the ways in which he has formed you, is forming you, and will form you.

In verse 11, the angels come to minister to Jesus once Satan has departed from him.

- In what ways has God ministered to you in difficult times?

- In what ways can you minister to those around you who are experiencing challenging seasons?

While this study is meant to help us see how the Bible speaks about the wilderness so that we can frame our own wilderness experiences properly, I also want us to see outside of ourselves. At Transformation Church we say, "Upward. Inward. Outward." This is part of our vision and is shorthand for saying, "Love God completely (upward), ourselves correctly (inward), and our neighbors compassionately (outward)."

One idea that has helped me in my own wilderness seasons is recognizing that I am not alone. We all encounter the wilderness in our lives. I believe that if we all took the time to look outward, God would give us opportunities to minister to one another and encourage each other to keep going. This is what the body of Christ is all about.

Write down an "upward, inward, outward" perspective on your most recent wilderness experience.

- ***Upward:*** How did God show up for you in this season?

- ***Inward:*** How were you transformed in this season?

- ***Outward:*** How will you encourage someone else as a result of this season?

PRAY

End your time today by thanking God for the upward, inward, and outward benefits of your wilderness experience.

DAY 4

READ & REFLECT

Read Matthew 27:45-50 and Luke 23:44-46

- Looking at both passages, what were the last two things Jesus ever said? In which order did he say them?

- How do you feel hearing Jesus' second-to-last statement? His last?

Jesus' entire life—in the wilderness, at dinner with friends, and out preaching in public—was framed by Scripture. He made sense of it all through the lens of Scripture. And in his last moments on earth, as he was suffering unimaginable pain, as people mocked him and encouraged him to save himself, he once again turned to the Word.

As a devout Jew, he would have memorized the entire book of Psalms, a book of prayers that had shaped the Jewish people for centuries. And in his moment of greatest anguish, it was those prayers that gave voice to both his pain and his hope.

When Jesus cries out, "My God, my God, why have you abandoned me?" he is quoting Psalm 22. All the Jewish people hearing him would have known immediately what he was referring to.

Read Psalm 22:1-5

- How does this passage give voice to anguish? Have you felt this way before?

- How does this passage maintain hope in the midst of anguish?

When Jesus cries out, "Father, into your hands I entrust my spirit," he is quoting Psalm 31:5. Again, this reference would have been recognized by his followers and other Jewish witnesses.

Read Psalm 31:1-5

- In what ways does this passage recognize the tragic nature of Jesus on the cross?

- How does the last line demonstrate Jesus' complete trust in God?

Throughout the six weeks of this study, we have seen how God can use the wilderness to help us grow strong in the spirit. Rooted firmly in the Word of God, Jesus was the perfect picture of spiritual strength, and his faith never wavered.

- How might God be inviting you to grow in new ways so your faith will sustain you throughout the trials and temptations of this world?

PRAY

As you finish today's study, take a few minutes to ask God to help you grow in faith, so it will mature and hold strong in the storms and difficulties of life.

DAY 5

REFLECTION DAY

Leaving the Wilderness (Luke 4:16-21)

Something I noticed throughout this week is that Jesus never lamented his time in the wilderness. He returned from the wilderness and started teaching. He knew the wilderness hadn't been a waste of time.

For the longest time I could not say the same. There were many times when I would remember a difficult situation or a harsh word or an offense against me and would immediately shut it out of my mind or curse it all over again.

I don't know the exact moment it happened, but I started feeling a stirring toward the end of 2017. I could sense God doing a new thing. A door I had been knocking on for a long time suddenly opened, but instead of stepping over the threshold, I stepped away and out of the wilderness.

Since I had graduated from seminary, it had been my dream to work full time at a church. I have a deep love for the local church. Hopefully you do too. That doesn't mean you have to work at a church—it just means you show a commitment to be an active member of the body. For me, I knew in my bones God was calling me to full-time ministry within the context of the local church, but there seemed to be a blockade. Although I had applied and been asked to apply for several positions, it never worked out.

Then one day, the small-groups director called me for a meeting. He wanted to offer me a job to work alongside him. I heard him out and recognized that this was just what I had been longing for. While I had been in the wilderness, however, God had changed my heart to lead me elsewhere. I ended up turning the job down. I thought I would feel awful, but instead I felt elated. I left that meeting feeling hopeful and expectant for God's plan to be revealed.

Within a matter of months God brought us to a new city, a new state, a new church—one with which my family and I aligned effortlessly. God had a better plan, and I could feel myself leaving the wilderness and entering a new season—the one God had been preparing me for all that time.

Because, remember, the wilderness is where God forms us, helping us grow strong in spirit.

Read Luke 4:14

Jesus returned in the power of the Spirit. That sounds like spiritual strength to me—the same strength John the Baptist displayed, the same strength available to us. Sometimes when we go through difficult circumstances, we learn how to cry out to God. We learn to depend on God for all our needs. We experience God in new and profound ways. But once those challenges pass, we get comfortable in our own adequacies. We start to forget—isn't that what the Israelites experienced as they took laps around the desert?

When we leave the wilderness, it's all the more important to continue relying on God and walking in the power of the Holy Spirit, as Jesus demonstrates. To keep developing that spiritual strength, reliance on the Holy Spirit.

Are you ready?

Looking back over the six weeks of study, how have you grown stronger spiritually? As a reminder, here are some of the highlights:

Week 1. The wilderness is an opportunity to develop the strength of relying on God and not yourself.

Week 2. The wilderness of oppression is an opportunity to develop the strength of trusting the Good Shepherd.

Week 3. The wilderness of sin is an opportunity to develop the strength of repentance.

Week 4. The wilderness of distraction is an opportunity to develop the strength of keeping your eyes on the cross.

Week 5. The wilderness of despair is an opportunity to develop the strength to receive nourishment, rest, and community.

Week 6. The wilderness of temptation is an opportunity to develop the strength of being armed with the Word.

Remember, you belong to Jesus and he has written your story to be one of triumph. Let's keep following the Spirit.

BENEDICTION

May the God of John the Baptist prepare you for your assignment on this earth.

May the God of Hagar see you with the same love and care with which he saw her.

May the God of Adam and Eve clothe you in love and righteousness.

May the God of Israel guide you back to him.

May the God of Elijah nurture and sustain you.

And may the Lord Jesus Christ be your ever-present hope as he provides a way through the wilderness. Amen.